Train of Thought

Daily Reflections & Recollections about Europe, Riding the Rails, Fast Food and Underwear...

...15 years after the fact

Tony Savageau

Walter Chalkley

Blue Mustang Press

Boston, Massachusetts

First printing

ISBN: 0-9759737-2-X
PUBLISHED BY BLUE MUSTANG PRESS
www.bluemustangpress.com
Boston, Massachusetts

Printed in the United States of America

Seeds from the Octopus's Garden, planted in soil of Monterosso, nurtured with liberal amounts of imagination yielded this trip. The solid memories that took root yielded this book.

To the FWAO, for whom this book chronicles not only an experience, but the culmination of intense friendship. It's a good thing we didn't know it was the last ride then, because something so sad could have spoiled a great trip.

Four days after they got off the train, the travelers separated. They have not been together in the same room since.

And, of course, to Karen and Melanie,
who, thank God, didn't know us then!

Train of Thought

Daily Reflections & Recollections about Europe, Riding the Rails, Fast Food and Underwear...

...15 years after the fact

Introduction: Tony

I was 13 years old and getting ready for one of my 8th grade basketball games at Lee Middle School in Grand Prairie, Texas. My dad came up to me and casually mentioned that he was being transferred on account of his job, and we'd be moving. I was stunned. My entire conscious life had been spent in Grand Prairie. I had known no other home. I was only a few months away from beginning my High School football freshman regimen. "Where are we going, Dad," was all I managed to ask.

"Germany," was his reply.

Germany? I was thinking Ft. Worth, Plano, maybe someplace really far away like, Waco. All towns located in Texas, but outside of Dallas County, where Grand Prairie was located. If I was stunned before, I was completely floored now.

I told a neighbor friend of mine that I was moving to Germany. She was surprised. I began to make my preparations. I would be leaving school a few weeks early to begin my journey to Germany, which included stops in North Dakota and Massachusetts to say goodbye to relatives. We were moving to Europe, after all. Way across the ocean.

Just a few days before we packed up and moved away from the only life I'd ever really known, I was talking to that same friend. I told her that I'd write after I got to Europe and...she interrupted me and said, "I thought you said you were moving to Germany?"

That was the moment I first thought to myself that seeing what life outside of

Grand Prairie, Texas was all about wasn't going to be as bad as I initially thought.

We arrived in Munich, West Germany in June of 1978. Shortly after arriving, I celebrated my 14th birthday and was given a Canon 35mm camera to help document my family's stay there. It's also when I began to chronicle my thoughts daily in a small, five year journal I'd received as a going away gift.

I entered Munich American High School that fall and began what I now fondly look back on as four glorious and character shaping years of my life. As a 14 year old, four years of my life represented almost 30% of my entire time on earth! And at times, I felt every minute of those four years. High drama experienced by most teens was not lost on me.

The unique experience of living in a foreign country, while attending an American school run by the Department of Defense offered many perspectives my friends in Texas could not begin to comprehend. Among them was getting used to the fact that your 'best friends' may up and move as quickly as their parents were transferred to another U.S. duty station, literally anywhere in the world.

But we endured and made do with whatever those pulling the strings thrust upon us. Eventually, a complicated series of events culminated in me being one fourth of a group that started hanging around together in the fall of 1980. Me, Dawn, Walter and Susi. I'm not sure any of us thought we'd end up spending so much time hanging out together, but the four of us practically moved around Munich as one. In fact, Walter moved in with my family our senior year of High School so he could finish his years at MAHS and graduate with us.

And the four of us had a blast. The closeness of our friendship eventually led to a thought. Wouldn't it be great to backpack through Europe together after we graduate from MAHS? We researched what it would take. Living in Europe, we opted to forego the popular U.S. based EurRail program and use the much cheaper InterRail program for Europeans. We began to save our money. We began to lay the groundwork with our parents. After all, what could be safer than four 17 year olds hopping the trains of Western Europe for a month? What was the big deal? We could handle it. And we'd do it on roughly $12 a day, per person.

We bought our backpacks. We practiced pitching our tents. We purchased a few basic supplies, but not too many, we'd figure things out as we went along, we had to travel light! We all had journals, to record our thoughts while we traveled. Finally, all of our parents agreed, some were more wary than others. I'm sure none of them had second thoughts!

We graduated MAHS on May 27, 1982. One of the quirks of the InterRail program was that you rode free on all participating countries rail systems *except* for the country in which you purchased your InterRail pass. Our early research had shown that our preferred route would not take us to Austria at all. On June 1, 1982 we hopped a train from Munich to Salzburg, Austria. We purchased our passes and ate lunch downtown. Then we jumped on the Munich bound train for one last night in Munich with our families and to say our goodbyes. We assured our moms, dads, brothers and sisters we'd be fine and that we'd keep in touch via post cards and maybe the occasional phone call (if the budget could stand it).

We decided to meet at Munich's main train station, the Hauptbahnhof, early on the morning of June 2. Looking like a group of climbers ready to take the summit of Mt. Everest, we boarded our train bound for Zurich, Switzerland. I always thought the Sherpa role was reserved for Walter.

You'll get an idea of what happened during that amazing month of June in 1982 as you thumb through *Train of Thought*. What may not be apparent is that within those amazing four years, the month we spent riding the rails of Western Europe had a profound influence on me for the rest of my life. I turned 18 during the final days of our trip. And I learned a lifetime of lessons about myself, about my friends, about the Europeans who welcomed and helped us throughout our journey, about my country and about what my place in the world could be, if I only tried.

Introduction: Butch

It was 1979 and we were going to Germany.

I didn't want to go to Germany. I fought it as much as a 14 year old could, which, really, isn't all that much. Fourteen year olds don't hold a lot of cards when it comes to making the big plays in families. Try as they might.

So I resigned myself to it and immediately set about making a plan for my return after one year. I had friends, I had school, I had a place. I didn't want to hear what a great experience this was going to be for me. I didn't want to hear the benefits of understanding another culture. I didn't want anything but to stay right where I was.

Well, it turns out that I didn't know what the hell I was talking about. I'm thinking it might be something to do with being 14, but who knows.

It turns out it *was* a great experience. Turned out to be one of the greatest actually. Despite not living in Germany on or even near a military base or being there in a military support capacity, I ended up going to school at Munich American High School. I lived in a small village about an hour outside of Munich and rode the metro (the s-bahn as it was called) into Munich most days, and rode it home every day. Students at MAHS in my situation were few and far between, most lived on base within walking distance of the school.

I was thrown into a culture I knew nothing about and slowly learned to make my way through it. It was frightening at first (as witnessed by a mistaken train ride to a town OTHER than the one I lived in with less than the German equivalent of $2 in my pocket) but slowly I got into it and found myself hanging out in downtown Munich much more often than I was at home.

The unprecedented freedom I had was amazing. The ability to take public transportation to within 500 yards of anywhere I wanted to be was amazing. The culture was amazing. The food was amazing. The BEER was amazing. And I loved it.

Perhaps even more amazing than that, I loved high school. I know…I know…I'm not supposed to love high school. It's supposed to be a time of high angst, full of sturm and drang, being tortured by bullies, trying to live up to your peers, and, of course, girls. Turns out it was a blast. I really can't think of many bad memories concerning school at all once I got to MAHS.

I have the benefit of having read Tony's intro before writing mine. What strikes me about his (aside from him calling me Walter…something he never did…something NO ONE ever did except a couple teachers) is his point about how friends could be transferred out of your life with very little notice. I can think of a couple of situations where someone told me their family was informed they would be transferred, and two weeks later they were gone. Usually it took longer than that, but the turnover was high. So you made friends quickly, and you tried to make them deeply, because anything could happen.

And it nearly did. Family upheavals left me with the prospect of leaving after my junior year. After dreading the thought of having to stay in Germany even one year, I was now dreading the thought of leaving after two.

I had friends, I had a school, I had a place.

And it turned out, this time, I really did.

Tony came to school one spring day in 1981 and walked up to me and said, "I talked to my mom, she said you could stay with us." I assumed he was talking about the coming weekend so I said, "Friday or Saturday?"

He laughed and said, "Next year."

Then he walked off to class.

I was floored. It was so totally out of left field I didn't know what to say or what to think really. I hadn't asked if I could stay and he had not mentioned anything about the possibility of me staying. But, as it turned out, I did stay. I didn't have to leave. I finished school there.

With my friends. At my school. In my place.

Over the intervening 24 years I've said thank you many times, but I always feel compelled to say it again. Thanks Tony — and thanks to Tony's family as well.

So, it came to pass that Tony and I both had girlfriends, Dawn and Susi, who also happened to be friends, and, as Tony described, we sort of all became inseparable. Perhaps too much so at times, but it could all be taken away at any second, so we stuck to each other like glue.

And, somewhere in there the idea popped up to do the train trip after graduation. Tony and I had done some backpacking and traveling in Italy and we decided it would be nice to extend that to the whole of Europe. Early drafts of the itinerary were wildly optimistic. Eastern Bloc (remember them?) countries were included, Greece, Scandinavia, and even Northern Africa made a very quick appearance.

The final list, the one we left Munich with folded in our back pockets was Switzerland, Lichtenstein, Italy, coastal France, Spain, Portugal, France, England, Scotland, Northern Ireland, the Republic of Ireland, Belgium, Holland, Norway, and then back down to Munich. Lichtenstein was an early casualty, Portugal lost out to a rainy night in Barcelona, and Norway was a victim of our own fatigue. But we did the rest. We spent 28 days traveling and living in EXTREMELY close quarters. And I loved every minute of it.

And then it was over.

Less than a week after the trip ended I left Germany. Everyone followed throughout that summer.

Susi and I moved to Virginia. Dawn and Tony went to school in New Hampshire. They split up. Then we split up. I haven't seen Susi since 1985. I've seen Dawn once since July of 1982. And I've seen Tony exactly twice. There were phone calls in those years, long ones. And then, when email came around, there was that, and I think that has helped the most. It was still sad, though, when I would stop and think about it, so I seldom did.

Until the summer of 1997 when Tony sent me an email with the subject line, "What were you doing 15 years ago today…?" and containing his journal entry for that day, 15 years ago. It was great. It was a wonderful relic. And it was so fun to read I just had to comment on it, dig out my journals, and send them on to him.

The commentary started out small and short. Just a small aside or something I remembered or something he remembered that didn't make the actual journal entry. Tony rarely commented on his journal entries before sending, I always did. Sometimes we would go back and forth for days on a particular entry, sometimes there would be hardly any discussion at all.

It was like taking the trip all over again, but this time from a couple different points of view. I not only got to see it from Tony's angle, I got to see it from MY angle…only a ME that was 15 years younger. It was revelatory. And it's something I would suggest everyone try.

So, here it is, all compiled together eight years after the fact. Why eight years? I don't know. Tony lost his copies of the emails. I lost most of mine with a corrupt disk. But it turns out I had forwarded my mom the emails as well and she had copies (thanks Mom!). It took forever to get them formatted, combine six days of back and forth emails into a page that resembled a conversation (difficult when some of the commentary was on other bits of commentary), and then move on to the next day which might be three or four days of back and forth emails.

To make matters even more complicated, Dawn joined the conversation near the end, much to our delight. Her commentary is illuminating as well, although, frankly, I'd like to see her and Susi's journals and see some commentary there as well.

That trip was important for all of us I think. *Looking back* on that trip fifteen years later was equally as important. If I were dictator of the world my first act (after lowering the retirement age to 29) would be to make such a trip mandatory for everyone graduating high school. I would make keeping a journal of such a trip mandatory as well. I would make it mandatory to drag those journals out every now and then and share them.

And I would make it mandatory to share them with me.

Tony and I will go first.

Here you go.

How to Read this Book

That may seem simple, but it's actually a bit harder than it looks.

First and foremost there are, in effect, five people talking within the text of this book. There is Tony in 1982 and Tony fifteen years later. There's Butch in 1982 and Butch fifteen years later. Then there's Dawn, one of the trip participants who got in on the modern day commentary towards the end.

Nature of the Commentary

All the commentary came from the bodies of emails which responded to bits of the journal entries, other commentary, and new topics. Sometimes these emails were exchanged simultaneously. All these emails were broken down and the chunks of commentary were placed in the narrative flow where they belonged. It is no exaggeration to say that two pages of commentary for an entry could have easily been ten or twelve email exchanges.

It works most of the time, but often questions weren't answered or there seems to be a bit of a bump in the narrative that doesn't make sense. This mostly happens in situations of "commentary on commentary" rather than "commentary on journal entries."

Who's Talking?

Originally we assumed we would use the drama convention for labeling who is talking by using tags such as "Tony82:" and "Butch97:" or something similar. However, often commentary interrupts a sentence and for it to work there should not be a label the reader has to essentially "jump over" so it was decided to do this with typeface with the exception of Dawn's commentary. Because she comes in at the end we have put the label "Dawn:" in front of her comments. We changed the typestyle as well.

For all other text in the book, the following rules apply:

•*TONY is always in italics: regular italics for his 1982 journal entry, **bold italics for his modern-day commentary.** This includes the journal entry heading.*

•BUTCH is always in regular typeface: again, regular for the 1982 entries, **bold for commentary.**

•Original 1982 entries are also indented.

•Dawn's commentary is in a different typeface, bold, and labeled.

Who's this Guy?

There is also the problem of names, or, rather, multiple names for one person. Walter Chalkley is also referred to as Mr. Bill and as Butch in the journal and in the commentary. Butch is a nickname Walter has had all his life, Mr.Bill was a nickname he picked up in Germany.

Tony called him "Mr. Bill" for the entire time he knew him in Germany but changed to calling him "Butch" on this train trip. You can see it happen in the journal entries. Early entries are all "Mr. Bill," later entries are "Butch." It could have been intentional. He still refers to him as "Mr. Bill" when speaking of him to others. Dawn did, and still does, call him "Mr. Bill," as can be seen in his commentary. For the sake of clarity, all headings are "Butch" (of course the cover says "Walter" – just to make it interesting).

What'd He Say?

Tony and Butch lived off the main military base in Munich so they spent a lot more time riding German public transportation, shopping in German stores, and interacting with other Germans than many folks who lived on base. As such, you will notice the occasional German word slip into the journal entries as it often crept into their everyday conversation (and, occasionally still does, when a German word says something better than an English word can). These will be translated as in parenthesis when they occur.

Extraneous Material

There are some other written materials listed in the journal entries, specifically Butch's. He has a listing for "Postcard" and another for "Marginal Notes."

As can be seen in the picture of Butch's Journal, the pages had blank margins on either side. Butch used them to jot down stray thoughts, exchange rates, beers sampled, and other comments. These are the "Marginal Notes."

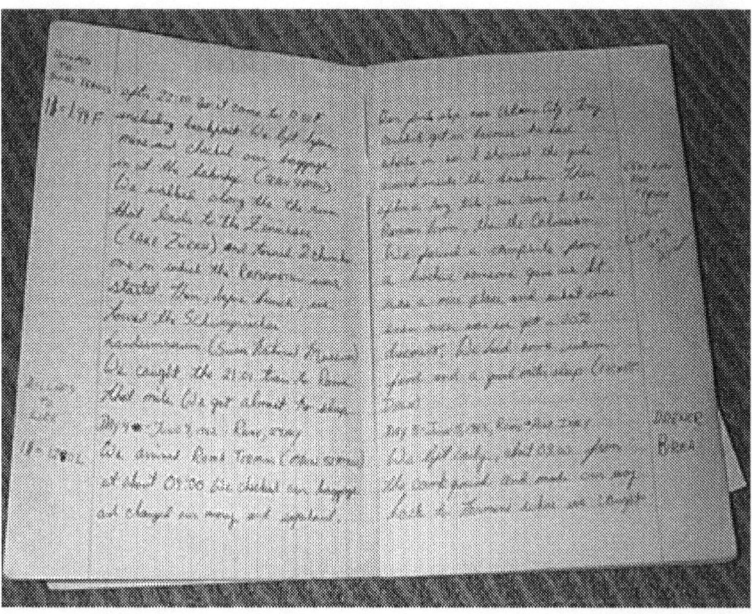

The "Postcards" were postcards Butch sent to himself. Whenever a batch of postcards were sent from a city to friends and relations, Butch would include one to himself with a brief outline of the current events on the back. He thought this would give him a nice picture, quick summary, stamp, and postmark from each country. Best of all, most of them were delivered. So, when Butch's journal mentions "Postcard," it usually describes the front and quotes the back.

We hope you enjoy this book, and be sure to check out the website, www.BlueMustangPress.com/train.htm for more info and pictures about this book.

All Aboard...!

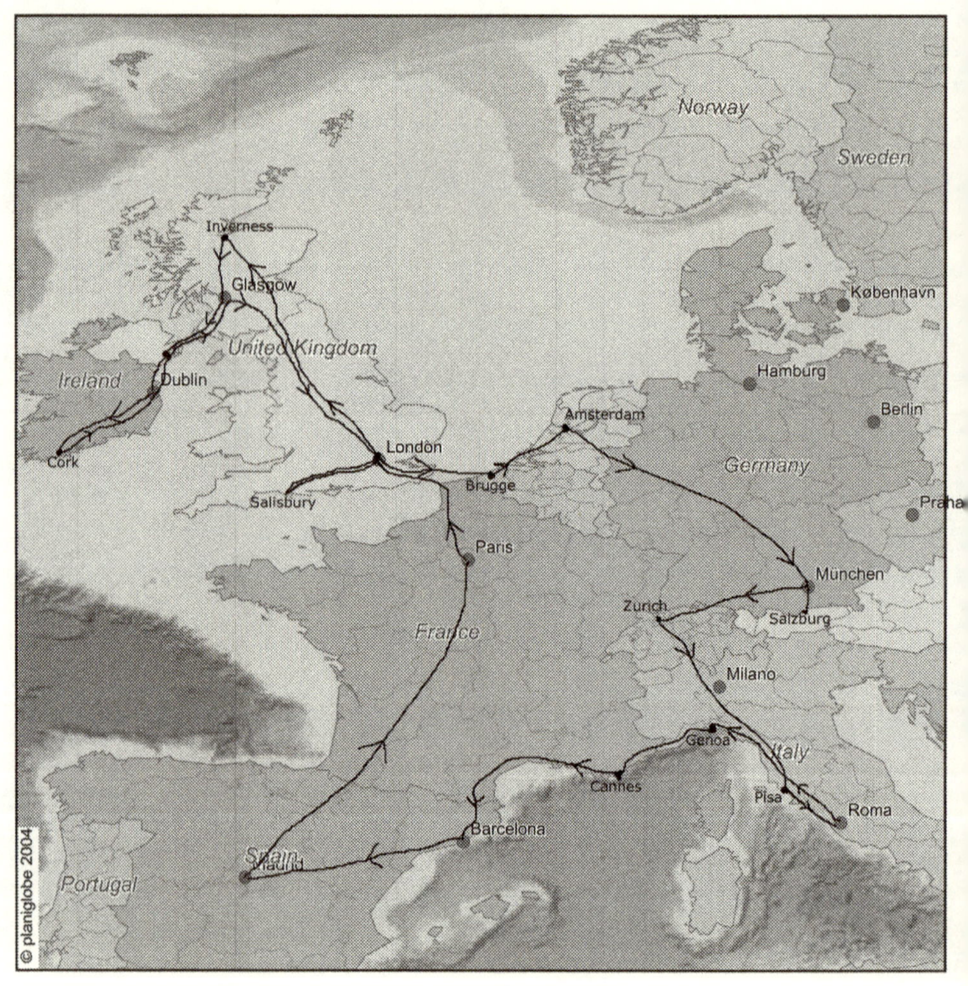

The Europe '82 InterRail Trip, June 1-28

Days: 28
Train Trips: 23
Countries: 11
Miles: 6200

Butch's Journal

Day 1 - June 1, 1982 - Salzburg, Austria

Went to Salzburg to buy our Interail tickets because we won't be doing any traveling in Austria.

Probably a bit of exposition Tony as I know your memory isn't what it once was: The way the Interail pass worked that made it different from the Eurail pass (which was frighteningly more expensive) was that it was good for free rail travel in all European countries (including the UK which the Eurail pass was not) EXCEPT the country in which you purchased it. In that country it was only good for half price. So, playing the system, as was our wont being anti-establishment youth, we bought a one-way ticket to Salzburg, right on the Austrian-German line, bought our tickets (which you could only buy if you had a European address....of which I had several by that point), walked around the city a bit, got back on the train and didn't have to pay a schilling, pfennig, or cent for the trip home. I've always been rather proud of our ticket buying legerdemain.

You see, this event obviously made more of an impression on you years later than the day it occurred. That's why I had no June 1 entry, bonehead. But I mean that in the nicest way!

And weren't we clever then though!

Arrived there from Munich at about 16:00 and left about 20:45. Returned to Munich.

Well, no use writing about a lot of stuff we didn't get to see anyway.

OK, off we go then, the rest of Europe to see and all. Tut-tut. Cheerio and all that. Well, we're off. Ta-ta.

POSTCARD: "A nice montage" of Zurich sights. Full of wondrous and glorious things that we didn't see. My note:

#1
Day One - First Stop - Hot - Having a good time - Pretty City - Didn't see much of it though.

I do remember we ate at a nice outdoor cafe. And from there we looked at the city. "Yep, there's the Hohensalzburg, and up there, those must be the salt mines, oh, and look, the Kapuzinerberg....finished eating? Well, let's go then."

Off to a very auspicious start...

Tony's Journal

June 2, 1982

Whoa whoa whoa. Hold on there Spanky. June 2nd?!? While I realize that was the first day WITH luggage, I don't think it can really count as the technical FIRST day of the trip. That would have to be Salzburg on June 1st....which is where MY journal begins.

The four of us got all things together and left for Zurich on time.

Probably the last time that would happen.

The train ride was very nice and comfortable.

Yes. A nice and comfortable train ride. Remember when we thought of train rides as "Nice and Comfortable"? "Why, we could just sleep here it's so nice and comfortable. It would save on accommodations."

We got into Zurich about ten minutes early, which was good.

Probably the last time for that too. It's that Swiss timekeeping you know.

At first we were going stay at a campsite, but decided against it because they didn't answer the phone.

Didn't we find out later that that campsite was in Zurich, Montana? It was 4 in the morning there, no wonder they didn't answer.

So, we stayed in a very nice youth hostel on the Morgenthal stop - SF 12.50 ($6.00) which included a shower and a breakfast.

Spending big bucks, worrying about showers boy what a bunch of virgins.

Tomorrow we explore Zurich. We're all tired now.

NOW??? TIRED NOW??!?!?!

Breakfast
SJH Zürich

*** 12.50← 01
-2VI88 4364 12.50TL 01

Butch's Journal

Day 2 and 3 - June 2-3, 1982 Zurich, Switzerland

Apparently I got a late start on this as this was a combined entry so I was writing it somewhere and at some time other than when it happened. Probably accounts for the lack of details.

Cheat, cheat, never beat...

We left Munich at 16:03 and arrived Zurich at about 20:45. The tourist office was little help except to give us a map and directions to the Zurich Jugendherberge (IYHF ***) the youth hostel in Zurich.

Sounds like a lot more help than we got at a lot of other tourist offices.

This must have left a monumental bad taste in our mouths because never again do we attempt to use the bureaucrats again on our trip. Well… except for every other time we went to tourist's offices for help…so I guess they weren't so bad. It must have been us!!

Arrived there at about 22:00, checked in and slept like a baby. Cost us 1f more because we checked in just after 22:00 so it came to 12.50f including breakfast. We left before 09:00 and checked our baggage in at the bahnhof (train station).

We walked along the river that leads to the Zurichsee (Lake Zurich) and toured 2 churches – one in which the Reformation was started.

Ok, I don't know where we got this information but I don't think it's correct. Martin Luther tacked up his thesis to the door of a church in Germany so we've lived that lie long enough I think.

Wasn't it John Calvin or somebody like that? I think this was the spot for the Swiss reformation. I know the Swiss had to be in on everything...until they became politically neutral and decided they could have twice as many deposits, I mean friends, that way.

Then, before lunch, we toured the Schweizrisches Landesmuseum (Swiss National Museum).

I have absolutely no recollection of this at all. None. Zip. Someone wanna help me out here and tell me something we might have seen?

I recorded it as well, but I don't remember anything about it. The one thing I do remember, I think, but didn't write about was the big vending machine wall. Was it in the train station? Remember? You could buy just about anything and it would plop down into your hot little hands. It was huge, about 20 by 50 or something like that. It's the first time I ever ate the world famous Swiss dehydrated train station fruit. We bought it out of this big thingy. Much more impressive than Calvinism and the Swiss Reformation.

ME TOO!!!!!! In fact, I've got a number of friends who are quite tired of hearing about the goddam vending machine. It was such a marvel of modern detached consumption that I'm amazed it wasn't here in America...or that I never saw another. It was entertainment and consumerism at its very best and I've always wanted to go back and see it (and the really sad part about this is that I'm not kidding in the least). Why didn't either of us record it in our journals? Was it a retrospective thrill? Was it that if there had been one of those in every train station we went to that we wouldn't have been as hungry? Not that there was just food in the thing, I'm remembering shirts, shoes cosmetics, laundry detergent (and not those little boxes you

get at the Laundromat either, I'm talking a big ass box of laundry detergent) and, apparently, dried fruit. I think we spent longer in front of the machine than we spent in Salzburg two days earlier.

We caught the 21:01 train to Rome that night. We got almost no sleep.

Poor babies. Obviously had not developed the talent of sleeping anywhere at any time yet.

Novices! We were still spoiled by the good life!

Marginal Notes: Dollars to Swiss Francs: $1=1.99sf

POSTCARD: A very nice view of Zurich with the river running through the middle and the big old Alps in the background. The note:

June 3, 1982
Stop #2
Hot Swiss Weather - Jugendherberg - Writing in the crypts

Remember this? The weather was so hot we plopped down in the crypts and wrote our postcards right beside this HUGE statue of Constantine that the curator tried to tell us was life-sized. "Hey, it's some Americans. Fritz, tell them that this is where the reformation started and that Constantine was really, really, big."

- Arrived late last night (21:00) - leave for Rome tonight (21:03)
- Two tower Church.

Butch' s Journal and the above-mentioned postcard

On the front of the postcard, off to the left is a two towered church. We were in the crypt of that church that we wrote our postcards while the HUGE eyes of Constantine looked down upon us.

Tony's Journal

June 3, 1982

Butch and I shared a room w/ six other dudes tonight.

Thought we had a room to ourselves. Did we talk to anyone?

It was a room with bunk beds. We pretty much kept to ourselves. Being the shy, American tourists we were.

I didn't sleep all that well though. We got up at 6:30 and took a shower and then ate. We checked out of the hostel by 9:00.

It took us two and a half hours to shower and eat? I remember that cafeteria breakfast, it's a wonder they even gave us a tray rather than have us just walk through the line and eat as we went. That's two and a half hours we could have been watching the vending machine.

We walked around the city to the lake. We saw the Fraumunster and Grossermunster churches. We also went to the museum.

Yeah, yeah. Churches, museum, check those off the list, OK, everybody on the train to Rome!

Zurich is really a nice, clean town and I encountered no hassles. Everybody was in good spirits all day. To tell the truth, we didn't really do very much to get tired, but we all were in a way.

BECAUSE WE WERE A BUNCH OF SISSIES!!! That's why!

I spent about $25 real easy here, too.

Glad we got out of those expensive countries early or this trip would have been over quick....(see "England").

No elaborate meals, but adequate.

Nothing like the fine McDining we would have later.

All in all I liked Zurich a lot because of its "friendliness". Now we are off for a ten hour train ride to Rome. Until then.

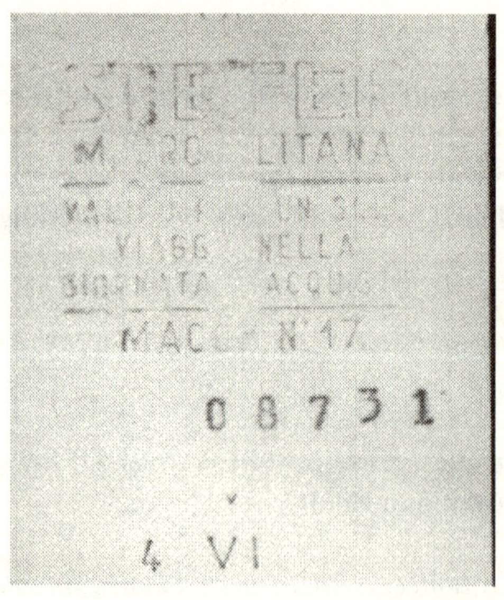

Tony's Journal

June 4, 1982

The train ride was twelve hours long and very uncomfortable. Nobody really got any decent rest so people were on edge.

I think this might translate as "Mr. Bill was getting on my goddam nerves." Or maybe I'm just being paranoid, which doesn't necessarily mean you weren't talking about me. It was day four. How were we on edge? I don't remember.

I didn't get to go into St. Peter's because I had shorts on.

Tony's shorts probably would have gotten him quick access to any bar down by the baths but, unfortunately, the Pope had certain standards to maintain.

It was a nice, sunny, hot day again.

It was a friggin' sunny, hot, MISERABLE day. I remember my arms got sunburned, it was muggy, and it was about 95 degrees in the shade.

We walked to the Roman Forum, the Colosseum, and then set out to look for a camp site. We found one about 10 mi. from the center of Rome.

Ummm....how did we get there?

№ 039855

INTER RAIL

2. Klasse

ÖSTERREICH

Gültig 1 Monat

vom 01 06 82 bis 30 06 82

Name SAVAGEAU, ANTHONY

Kontrolle	Datum	Von	nach
	01.06.82	Salzburg	München
	über		
	02.06.82	München	Zürich
	über		
	03/4.06.82	Zürich	Roma
	über	CHIASSO	MILANO
	05.06.82	Roma	Pisa
	über		
	06.06.82	Pisa	Genoa
	über		

Tony's InterRail pass book and the first leg of the trip - the destinations were written in by us and validated by the conductor on the train.

By bus. If it wasn't a train or walking...it was a bus!!

It's pretty nice and costs about $3.00 per person (650 IL for two). It began to rain a little bit, but nothing drastic. Everybody took a shower and Dawn feels "200%" better. I sure do.

Oh, come on guys, it's only day four, you had a shower the previous day, and I doubt it was time to change Tony's underwear yet. How could you feel so much better? I mean, my god, we were at home the day before YESTERDAY!

We sat around our site talking and planning for the trip.

Because, as everyone knows, four days into your trip is the best time to start planning.

Our next halt (stop)

Remnants of the S-Bahn culture we lived and breathed.

is to be Pisa, hopefully.

Butch's Journal

Day 4 - June 4, 1982 - Rome, Italy

We arrived Roma Termini (main station) at about 09:00. We checked our baggage and changed our money and explored. Our first stop was Vatican City, Tony couldn't get in because he had shorts on

A little consistency in our journals is nice.

Another thing that stands out in my memory, yet we failed to mention, is that this was our first experience with an Inter Rail surcharge. Remember? We had to fork over a little extra cash because we were on a "Speedy Train" from Switzerland. I remember the Italian conductor trying to explain it all to us, and the speedy train was born. I still use that expression today whenever I'm on an express train (since I've been commuting to Boston every day for the last three years I get to say this a lot, but I'm the only one that still laughs). I've got pictures of us in St. Peter's feeding our first set of Pigeons. I'm in my sexy shorts (oh to have those gams today!), with my Gopher hat, and ultimately cool brown walking shoes.

so I showed the girls around inside the basilica.

Because, you know I had been there many times before because JP2 and I were tight, best of buds, so I figured I should show them all the hot spots inside the basilica. I think, actually, I had been there before and knew what boring stuff to skip.

And I'm hanging out in the square trying to talk it up with the Swiss guards, you know, "So, do you miss home? We were just in Zurich, nice town, great vending machines, etc."

Then, after a long trek, we came to the Roman Forum, then the Colosseum. We found a campsite from a brochure someone gave us. It was a nice place and what was even nicer was we got a 20% discount.

MARGINAL NOTE: 6500 Lire for 2 people and one tent with 20% discount.

Explain to me why I was so god awful impressed with this sixty cent discount.

But as we'll come to see, that sixty cents will mean the world to you in Scotland!! This is the only place we stayed that I have almost no memory of at all. It just isn't clicking in.

OK, regular American style campground, big hill behind us leading up to somewhere where we washed our dishes from dinner that night. That's about all I can remember.

We had some warm food and a good nite's sleep (except Dawn).

Now there's a real shocker.

MARGINAL NOTES: Dollars to Lire $1= 1280 lire

POSTCARDS: I've got four, count 'em, FOUR cards for this day. Two of them were shitty little freebie postcards from our campground (Camping Nomentano, Roma, Tel. 06/6100296) that I didn't send. They are both pretty much the same, scenes of the camp snack bar, ping pong table, and some very hip folks doing very hip folk things

like writing postcards and walking in front of the snack bar (which must be a really hip thing to do as this same picture is on both postcards).

One of the other postcards is of the Colosseum and on the back I wrote:

June 4, 1982 - #4
Hot - hot - hot- Colosseum nice but overrated

What a spoiled little American shit I was.

What's two thousand years of history when Virginia and Mass have been kicking back for about 300 years, ruling the world.

- going camping now - then go swimming.

Now I'm starting to remember the swimming part was just a scam, I don't recall any pool or swimming or anything.

The other postcard is of the Vatican and St. Peter's Square mailed with a Vatican stamp and postmark. I wrote:

June 4, 1982
Rough Train Ride - Hot

"Hot" seems to be a recurring motif here.

- camp tonight - going inside now where it's cool

plan of the city
ROMA
E.N.I.T.
Italian State
Tourist Department

Tony's Journal

June 5, 1982

We left Rome at about noon for Pisa. We had a good night's sleep and a pretty decent breakfast.

I like it better when we keep track of everything we ate. I can't wait until we start stuffing ourselves with Burger King and other McGoodness so we don't actually have to think about what we might have eaten. No mystery at all. Not like "Oh, a KFC...I wonder what they serve there?"

The train wasn't too bad. We all slept most of the way, for the most part.

Because of all that boring Italian countryside. Who wants to see that anyway?

We got to Pisa around four o'clock. The leaning tower was a sight to see, but it was closed off because of a worker's strike.

Damn unions.

No big problems yet. Susi has a few pangs of something every now and then.

As she did for the four years I knew her.

Dawn had a splinter or two, so far.

Probably from all the hiking in woodland areas we were doing. WHERE THE HELL DID YOU GET SPLINTERS FROM DAWN?

Mr. Bill and I haven't really had any ills to speak of, yet.

Can't wait until I get my rash and give you something to talk about.

Me either!!

We are camping about 2 Km from the tower and it's fairly nice.

Was it that far? I seem to remember it being real close. Actually, in my memory we camped right under the tower but I kind of figured that wasn't right.

About 3000 IL ($3.00) per person for this place. We had an OK dinner and will be taking showers early tomorrow and head for a rest in Genoa.

Showers, showers, showers. I'm glad we got over all this shower and personal cleanliness further on in the trip.

Well, it was about 100 degrees in Italy. But Dawn looked very comfortable in her corduroys at the Vatican.

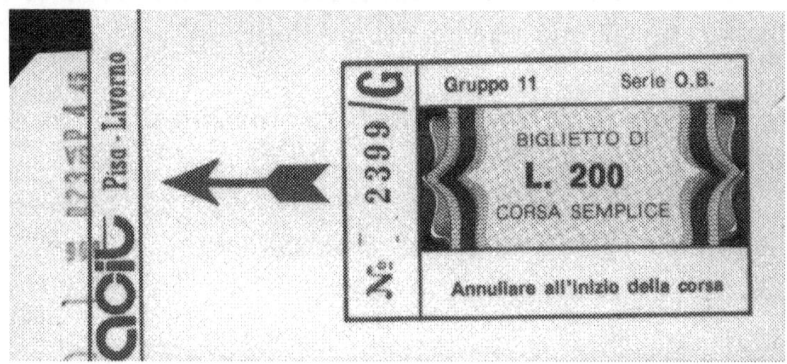

Butch's Journal

Day 5 - June 5, 1982 - Rome to Pisa, Italy

We left early, about 09:00 from the campground and made our way back to Termini where we caught the 12:00 train to Pisa. We got to Pisa around 16:00. The tower was closed so we just walked around it. LET'S GO suggested a campground so we tried it.

I remember this place quite clearly. It was fairly crowded as I remember and it was all young people, not much older than us. Mostly hippies. Throwing Frisbee, playing music, 3 days of Peace, Love, and Music....no, wait, that was somewhere else.

After Zurich, this is the place where I remember staying next. It wasn't bad. I do have a couple of pictures of three of us standing in front of the leaning tower. We have our packs on. One is a 'normal' picture. The other is of us 'leaning' as if to correct the tower's lean. Who said we didn't keep our sense of humor on this trip!

Were we some wacky kids or what...and the best part is we were probably the only people who EVER did that!

I'm sure we could have trademarked it or something...if we had a little more discretionary lira.

For 2 people it came to 5600Lire. Not bad.

Apparently we didn't get a coupon to knock off that half a buck we got in Rome.

We had another warm meal and a fairly restful night.

MARGINAL NOTE: Only one, a rather cryptic scrawling in the margin that says only:
Drener Birra

Near as I can tell it was a beer I had. I do remember buying one in the camp store but, as I didn't rate it like I did other beers in the journal, I either had not begun to rate the beers or it sucked.

I remember this beer. It wasn't that good. It's only become apparent to me after re-reading the entries how an important part of this trip was spent sampling the local brews. It must have been that Bavarian influence.

And it's still something I try to do. I'm amazed you remember the beer itself, I really don't.

I was amazing…less so now, just in case you're wondering.

POSTCARD: A typical postcard from Pisa. A shot of the tower and a shot of the grounds around the tower (with the tower in it, so that's two, count 'em, TWO shots of the tower on one postcard...what a bargain). On the back I wrote:

June 5, 1982
Everything great - Still hot - Camping last night (Rome) great place – Tower closed - maybe tomorrow - Camping tonight and hot meal

That's twice I've mentioned a hot meal. I don't recall us being quite so picky about the temperature (or even the thoroughness of the cooking) of meals in later locales.

As if the Ezbits weren't enough...

But, you know, when is the Ezbits ever really enough?

- Showers last night, first time in 2 days.

I laugh at our pampered lifestyle.

Wacky teenagers -Susi, Butch, Tony - leaning into it.

Tony's Journal

June 6, 1982

We left Pisa campsite pretty early to get to Genova.

Why were we in an all fired hurry to go to Genova? There was nothing there, we didn't go anywhere or see anything, so why did we stop there at all? I sure hope it wasn't my idea.

Sausage or Salami was probably the bigger motivator.

> *We got there at about 1 p.m. and found out our campsite was 45 minutes in the direction we had just come. We got to Rapallo and walked around to find our campsite. It certainly wasn't what the book said it was going to be.*

I go into this in a tad more detail in my entry for this day.

> *We have been taking it easy today for the most part except for a walk to the harbor. We cooked spaghetti which turned out to be rather funny the way it came out.*

I think "crunchy" would have been a better word than "funny". Or, perhaps, sticking with the classics and just saying "bad" would have been better.

> *Took some showers and really haven't been doing anything today.*

See, why we didn't take many showers at the end of the trip is that we took a lot at the beginning and saved them up. I remember in Scotland Tony saying to me, "I was going to take a shower this morning but I remember I took that extra one back in Genova so I don't need one."

We hope to get to Cannes by tomorrow afternoon. Mr. Bill believes there will be no problem in getting there in time to sun bathe.

Cup half full....

I, however, have my doubts.

......and half empty. (but, in this case, correct)

No tensions between anyone, to speak of.

No, but you're poised and ready aren't you?

It's in my nature...what can I say?

We hope to get an early start tomorrow. We'll see.

Zurich Youth Hostel - 20 MIN FROM HBF, (NOT 45) and is open until 1:AM FOR CHECKINS. [struck out] + IF AFTER 10:00

CAMPING NOMENTANO - ROMA - VIA della Cesarina 2 - TEL 06/610 02 96 - NICE PLACE - FRIENDLY MANAGEMENT - GENERAL STORE - DAY ROOMS, SNACK BAR, NICE SHOWERS & WC. TAKE BUS 36 FROM TERMINI TO PLAZA SIMPIONE WHEN YOU GET OFF THE BUS TURN RIGHT THEN LEFT, [struck out] FROM THERE CATCH BUS 337 TO THE CAMP Person/nite L3200 TENT/NITE L1700

CAMPING MIRA FLORES - only if you're hard up for accomodation. 3000/person/nite 2000/tent/nite. RAPALLO - 30 min south of Genova. From RAPALLO train station take Bus San Piedro to St. Anna. Stay on right hand side of road. Nice management / open fire grill, over grown and ground rocky, not near what it says it is near. Camping in RAPALLO Also accross the street and about 1 km down that road.

Back page of the "Let's Go" book - short reviews of the places we stayed for the "next time" we did the trip.

Butch's Journal

Day 6 - June 6, 1982 - Pisa to Genoa (Rapallo)

We left early - about 08:30 to catch the 10:41 train to Genoa. We got there then had to come back about 30km to Rapallo where this really good campground was. It was a let down,

"a let down"....sheesh, always the master of understatement. I remember this place being a hole. I couldn't believe how off the *LET'S GO* book was. I think the owners must have bribed whatever Harvard student wrote that review.

Yeah, it was nothing to write home about. I remember having to walk up a big hill to finally get to the entrance. Rapallo does make it on the maps of Italy I've seen though. We should have headed a little further south and stayed in Monterosso for old time's sake. As I remember, we may have even suggested that to the women and got the quick veto. You had to be there to really appreciate the rock we stayed on there.

Well, after all we went through to get to that rock we had better appreciate it. I left my umbrella there when we evacuated during the monsoon (all great campers carry umbrellas you know) I've always wondered if it was still there as our site was not too accessible. I also left a pair of socks there...but then, I wouldn't have WANTED to carry those home if you remember (in case you don't, here's a hint: we forgot to pack toilet paper).

crappy place, rocky and not near anything. We made spaghetti, I've had better but it was OK.

Just call me Pollyanna. Putting that positive spin on crunchy spaghetti. I do remember this meal quite well though. We bought all the stuff at the camp store, and we each bought a part of it since we were all going to eat it (although, thinking back on it, I think it would have been really nice of Dawn to spring for the whole thing as she had about a jillion dollars at this point....but I digress) and we cooked it on the camp's grill....but I don't remember what we used for fuel. Did we buy charcoal or did we break up some of the camp furniture? Help me out here.

I've got a good memory of this banquet feast. We did the good thing and gathered up sticks and brush from around the site. Got things started with our ever present, yet infrequently mentioned Ezbits.

You know, I was thinking about that too. I never mention the thing yet we use it quite a lot during the first part of the trip (I think the hostels would have frowned on its usage later on) Do you still have it? I've been looking for one for years because I was amazed how well it worked. Let's pause now to acknowledge the Ezbits....

.....Ok, that's enough.

We had a roaring flame going. Remember? We had a set of nice, new cook pots for our trip, although I don't remember who carried them.

You know, I may be wrong on this, but I think we took turns carrying them...really. I think we did. We were trying to create a new and better egalitarian society out there and we each carried the pots. You know, to each according to his needs (of which I have many) from each according to his abilities (of which I have few). Of course,

I could be way wrong on that as I haven't thought of the pots in years.

By the time we were done, we had charred that baby black because the flames were licking up all over the place. And those pots came in handy later on in Spain.

I remember the black soot as well, as I recall we didn't bring dishwashing soap, right? We used sand, right? Am I remembering that correctly or was that an episode of *Little House on the Prairie* or something?

Not being ones to think ahead that well, it was only after the inferno started that we realized we had no way to get the pot off of the grill, especially with flames shooting about three feet into the air. I think we rigged another stick through the handle of the pot and finally got it off the flame. I don't think the pasta was cooked through completely,

Not just crunchy because of that, but also because we didn't break the pasta and the ends were sticking out of the side of the pot and, what with the small brush fire we had started, we couldn't get our hands safely through to push it all under the water. Therefore the ends were quite...well...let's say "toasted" to be nicely understated.

but it was our first true camp cooked meal.

And our last endeavor of such magnitude.

We went to bed kinda early, about 22:00.

MARGINAL NOTES: Merely the price of this wonderful campsite: 8000 Lire per night.

What a gouge!!! However, I don't make note if that was for all of us, two of us, or just one, so I guess it could actually have been a bargain.

No matter the cost, it was overpriced.

POSTCARD: "A nice montage" of Rapallo with the words "Saluti da Rapallo" meaning, I guess, "Thanks for Coming to Rapallo Suckers" but it's hard to imagine this place being anyone's destination (of course, it was ours for some reason). The pics on the front show crowded beaches and full harbors of sail boats. None of which I remember seeing in Rapallo. On the back I wrote:

> #6 June 6, 1982
> Still hot - Crappy campsite - Can't swim - Water too trashy and you have to pay -

I remember this really shocking me because I had never been to a beach where you had to pay to use. Also, I remember thinking that if you were going to pay to use something like a beach they should at least clean out the garbage before asking you for your dough.

That whole place was one of those that the Let's Go folks must not have visited in person within the last...ten years! It was probably here that I lost faith in the book and abdicated tour guide responsibility to Butch.

> Bought Spaghetti to fix tonight - Genoa and Cannes tomorrow - Barcelona the next 4.

Tony's Journal

June 7, 1982

Today was really a wasted day.

Not to jump ahead here but my entry for this day begins, "Pretty much a wasted day."

....I guess it really was.

We left our camp in Rapallo early, but there were no trains to Cannes until 15:29. So we had about a three hour wait at the Genova P.P. We played cards and Mastermind. We got into Cannes at about 8:30 p.m. and we walked to the beach and sat there and watched the waves for about fifteen minutes.

"Ok, check Cannes and the French Riviera off the list, c'mon, c'mon, we're in a hurry here. Spain next right?"

I think we hoped to see more than waves. We'd heard so much about the swim wear at Cannes...or really, the lack thereof. I'd hoped it would be like watching the sunbathers at the Isar all over again! But it must have been too late.

We are catching the 22:52 train to Port Bou, Spain tonight in the hopes of reaching Barcelona by mid morning on the 8th. I think we can do it OK. That's about it, I guess.

You seem a little disappointed here. Like we shouldn't have wasted a day. Like it wasn't the first of several wasted days.

We had pizza and crap for lunch in Genova.

Believe it or not I remember this for some reason. The pizzas were individual size and they had slices of tomato on the top. Too weird that I remember it.

No one has gone hungry yet.

Plenty of time for that.

Everyone is looking forward to the beaches in Spain and a little sun.

Oh, "looking forward" to it now are ye? And in a week you're dissing it up and down.

I almost forgot to mention the really strange people we saw in Cannes. Some 'interesting characters' all up and down that stretch of sand including drug dealers, in fact; one man came up to us and pointedly asked if we smoked hash. It was pretty funny.

I've got a pretty good account of this as well in my journal.

Blatt 2

Kontrolle	Datum	Von	nach
	06.06.82	GENOVA	RAPALLO
		über	
	07.06.82	RAPALLO	Cannes
		über GENOVA	VENTIMIGLIA
	07/08.06.82	CANNES	BARCELONA
		über PORT BOU	
11 JUN 1982 BARCELONA		Barcelona	Madrid
		über	
1982		Mad	Paris
		über	

Tony's InterRail pass book - leg 2

Butch's Journal

Day 7 - June 7, 1982 - Rappalo to Genova, Italy to Cannes, France.

Pretty much a wasted day. Left Miraflores about 08:30 got to Genova BR about 10:00 - Genova PP about 10:15.

We knew the difference between the right and wrong train station in Italy, how did we forget it in Spain?

It's just a way to keep the tourists on their toes.

We checked times, ate the best pizza in Italy

I don't know if this was our designation or theirs but, as noted in my commentary to Tony's journal, it was quite tasty.

I don't think I would have called this the best pizza in Italy. In fact, most of the pizza I'd ever had in Italy was pretty bland. But I never sent anything back to the kitchen, mind you.

Yeah, perhaps, but I do remember this being pretty good train station pizza.

and waited. The first train we missed because there wasn't enough room. The next one, at 15:39 took us to Cannes.

So, basic translation: We hung around the Genova train station for FIVE hours.

As we had learned in our first Italy trip the year before, hanging around train stations can be a pretty good life, until they kick you out.

And provided you've mastered the technique of sleeping with one eye open and waking up every eight minutes to make sure you still have all your belongings.

> It was late by the time we got there, about 20:30. We walked down to the beach and watched the people.

Notice not a single euphemism.

You've always been a little more left of center than I.

I remember once making a very similar remark to you and you got fairly offended. Of course, I may have referred to the left as "enlightened" and the right as "fascist" but it's pretty much the same thing...tomato tomato.

> Then went back to the train station. Met this guy who just got robbed. He hinted for money but we didn't have any to give him.

Thank GOD! I think about this now and wonder if I was ever that trusting or if I've just become cynical. He was well dressed, well spoken, and American and he needed to bum money from US? I remember feeling really bad for him and wishing I could give him some dough, and then feeling bad later that I didn't give him SOMETHING, a couple of bucks, anything. I'd like to find this piece of shit and give him something now.

I didn't remember the part about him being robbed. I didn't think he was American either. I guess I was more afraid of interesting people and drug dealers stalking us...

Really? You don't remember him being American? Maybe he wasn't. I would hate to think I've carried that false memory for all these years. I guess I didn't say he was American in the journal entry did I? I do remember him saying he had been robbed however because I was considering giving him dough.

We caught the 22:52 to Barcelona.

And Tony's favorite part of the trip.

Now, now. Lest you think I'm anti-Spanish or something let me set the record straight. I liked Spain, OK? I just think we spent two days too long there, that's all. After all, we did finally get to a KFC here, you gotta like that.

Yes...the beginning of the fast food frenzy.

MARGINAL NOTE: A little drug humor:

We also were asked if we spoke English. When we said "yes" he asked if we smoked hash. He was very disappointed when he found out we "smoke nothing."

I'm surprised I even note this as often and in as many countries as it happened to me (must have been the hair). I think I remember this mainly because of the shock in the guy's voice while saying "You smoke NOTHING?" But, I also remember this happening a number of times in Munich ("You are American?" "Yes." "Oh...You have shit?") and, Tony, surely you recall our spring trip to Italy the year before when it seemed to happen every 15 minutes.

Oh yeah, we just tip-toed through Europe living among the drug elite. Drugs, Americans, c'mon it's like mom and apple pie.

POSTCARD: The last of many postcards from Italy. This one from Genova. A very nice montage of two sites from Genova that, since we never left the train station, we didn't see. On the back I wrote:

#7 June 7, 1982
Still hot - might camp in Cannes - Depends on what time we get there – Need some sun and beach

I think someone else must have written this postcard because I can't think of a time now when I would have actually felt I NEEDED two things I dislike so much.

- No swimming yet

I didn't realize how big your hankering was for a swim. It must have started sometime in Italy, because you've mentioned it a few times over the last couple of days' entries. Well, as we'll see, that Spanish sun fixed you on day one!

Oh yes. At the time I really loved swimming, and therefore, really loved the beach. However, as I became an adult, I realized that a trip to the beach was expensive, a marvel of logistics, sandy, and, more often than not, I ended up burned and throwing up from sun poisoning by the end of the day. Give me a pool, a nice indoor pool, or, lacking that, at least a pool very near the indoors so that I may swim and then retreat as needed. That, my sun-baked friends, is the good life.

Tony's Journal

June 8, 1982

The train ride was pretty long and I didn't get too much sleep till after we passed Marseilles.

Wasn't that three stops away?

When we got to Port Bou, we switched trains and rode for two hours to Barcelona. We got there in the morning but it took us a while to walk through what seemed half the city before we found the bus that took us to a campsite area.

Really? I guess I remember walking through the city…but it didn't seem like that long. I do NOT remember the bus ride though.

We had Kentucky Fried Chicken for lunch.

And I would have licked my fingers except I used the bathroom on the train.

After that we walked quite a ways looking for a campsite Susi knew.

"Quite a ways" – very nice understatement…I think we nearly walked back to Port Bou, no?

We settled on a different one which costs about 250 Pesetas per person per night ($2.45).

Hey, big spender!

It is the best of the campsites, so far, in our trip.

Without a doubt…I could have lived there I'm sure.

Plenty of shade, big store, nice bathroom facilities and a very good beach only about 250 yards down the road.

Road? What road? I thought it was a walk straight from our tent to the beach.

We plan to stay here for three nights and on the fourth day go to Madrid.

See, you should have never written it down. Once you wrote it down you could never forgive the Spanish weather for breaking up your precious schedule.

We did our wash and it was hilarious. Four people used 100 ft. of rope when hanging our stuff to dry. We have cordoned off our campsite like West Berlin. We all got burned a little at the beach, Mr. Bill more than anyone.

There's a shocker!

We are all gonna be really dark in three days. Mr. Bill and I hunted crabs and periwinkles in the Mediterranean and it was pretty fun.

It was. I always enjoyed hunting very small shellfish.

Looking forward to a good night's sleep here tonight and a chance to really *relax.*

See, and yet when given a chance to have an extra day of such wonderful surroundings, you opted to bitch for the rest of the trip! Careful what you wish for buddy.

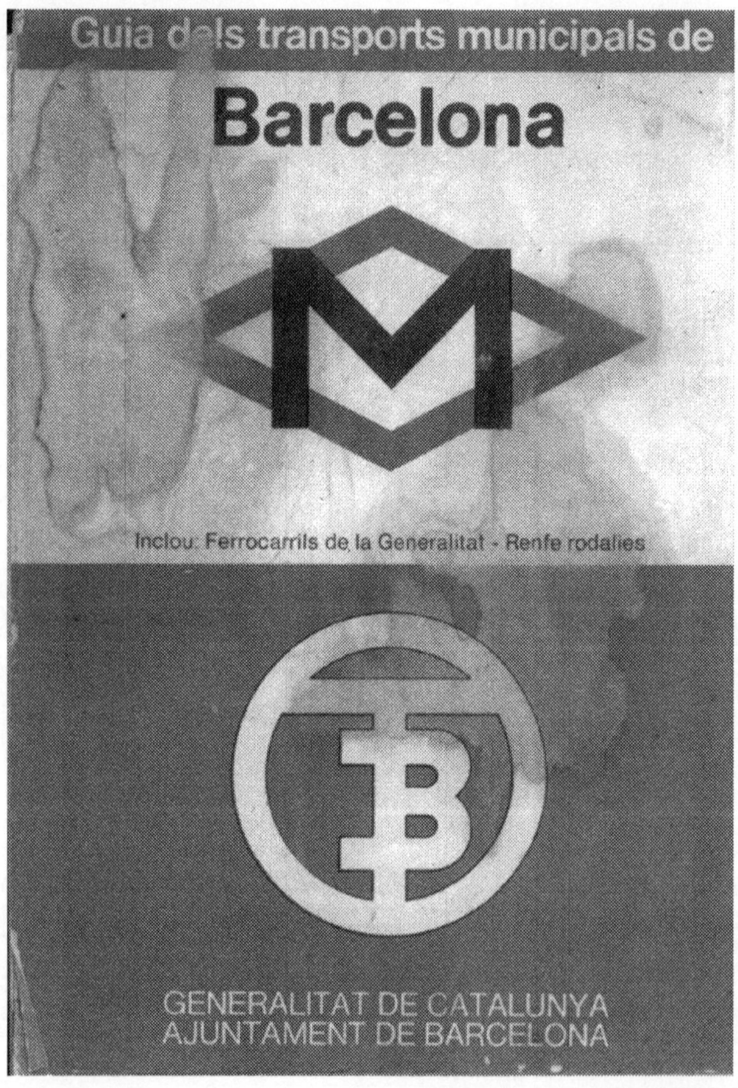

Butch's Journal

Day 8 - June 8, 1982 - Barcelona, Spain

At Last.

Similar to Tony's thoughts when we *left*.

We got here about 09:30. We tried to get help from the tourist offices but they kept giving us the run around. After much trouble we finally got there. Found the right bus, and got off about 2km away from where we eventually camped. We camped at a place 200m from where we wanted to camp.

Boy, it's a good thing I've got some memory left or that would make no sense. If I recall, and I think Tony mentioned something about it in his journal, we were looking for a place that Susi and her family had stayed at the previous summer. Susi claimed it was fantastic and we were searching for it, but, as I remember, she had forgotten what the name of the place was. We finally said screw it and took the next place that we found, only to find out later when we were walking around that the place we were looking for was only another 200meters away. And didn't look that much different.

I think that's it. We were looking forward to lavish beaches, hot meals, nude women (we'd missed them in Cannes after all), good music, all the stuff Susi experienced the year before. We might have had that had we walked a little further. We'll never know. It only

looked the same, but I'll bet the experience within was TOTALLY different...

> Doesn't matter, It's a nice place, management is nice and the beach is 100m away. When we finally made camp, and ate our KFC,

Now, I'm not one to argue with myself (oh, you are too!) but didn't we eat our KFC while we were still LOOKING for the place to camp? I remember sitting in a little grove of trees, on our packs, sweating like hogs, eating our KFC because we were starving and, apparently, never going to find our campsite. Is this right? Does anyone else remember it that way or do we eat it at camp as is implied in my journal? Or, better question, does everyone else still have a life and not worry about details like that?

You're right. We didn't eat our KFC at the camp. I seem to remember getting it before we got on the bus, carrying it with us (fighting off hoards of hungry Spaniards eager for a taste of America) and settling down to eat before we camped. It's details like these that will keep us off of the Alzheimer medication for at least a few years longer. Or keep running this through your head when next being tortured by enemies of the U.S., doesn't that happen a lot to you guys?

> we went down to the beach and I got burned to a crisp, but it doesn't hurt.

Oooooo, big man. Let's hear the talk when you're rolling around in agony later that night because your chest itches and you can't scratch your broiled skin.

It was early in the trip, you had to be brave. We didn't want the women to worry! You had gotten singed a bit in Rome, so who can blame you for trying to put on a brave face (at least to yourself, wussy).

We showered,

Jeeeze, it's like all we did was shower.

It was all due to the climate, once we got up North where it was 40 degrees and the sun didn't set we began to see why the folks in the middle ages never bathed!!

ate, and washed clothes. We have 100ft of clothesline strung around our camp, it looks like a gypsy camp.

Uh-oh. There's my non-PC reference. They're gonna take away my ACLU card now.

Remember, you were only in high school. You hadn't been exposed the liberal leaning institutions of higher learning in the U.S. yet. What did we do with that rope? It never gets mentioned again. Do you remember?

Our place is the best,

Yeah, it's way cool.

We Americans are really very territorial. We staked our claim to our space and we didn't want no stinking outsiders to wander through. I'm pretty sure we always had someone stand guard...I'm sure we were very popular here...I wonder why nobody talked to us??

it's shady and no one is near except 2 guys and they don't bother us.

I see, there's NO ONE *except* 2 guys. Well, that would be more then wouldn't it?

Everybody else was up the road at Susi's old place, having a grand time with the King of Spain. We were starting to figure out what sea life we could eat without keeling over with Hepatitis. You know, I had a blood test and I had to fess up to the Doc that I ate crustaceans out of the Mediterranean when I was 17 and if anything weird showed up, it was probably because of those critters. He didn't think that would have bothered me as long as everyone washed their hands after going to the bathroom and before we ate. (Yeah, right, and this guy went to med school for a hundred years for that bit of advice).

> Cheap place too, only 1080pta for four people and 2 tents per night. Cheapest place yet. The showers aren't really hot and the bathrooms leave a little to be desired

Good lord, what must they have looked like for ME to make that observation?

As much as we dissed Rapollo, I do remember the bathrooms being pretty nice. We were ready for luxury. The NICER johns were up the road at Susi's old place, I'm positive.

> but they're better than anything we've stayed in yet, except maybe Rome,

Hmmmmm, they're the BEST, EXCEPT this other place.

I do this for the whole journal, ***except*** **for the rest of the entries.**

When you get right down to it, there's really no better time or place to be than the moment in which you are living. Now, if you'll come with me to Mr. Coulter's room, I'll just start to write random thoughts on the board and try to be much more profound than I ever could be (I still do that once in awhile at my office on the white board, the execs look in and think I'm really busy, but I'm just having a good time, it helps me think).

and at these prices, I'm not complaining.

MARGINAL NOTE: Just a couple: the exchange rate: $1=102pta and a two star rating for Skol Beer, apparently a Spanish beer that I don't remember drinking.

Susi, Butch, Tony - at rest - note fast food debris strewn about

Tony's Journal

June 9, 1982

Mr. Bill had to wear a shirt because he got burned pretty good yesterday.

The more things change the more they stay the same. I would bet that over the 15 summers between then and now I've probably overburned myself 14 times. A normal person would have given up.

And why did this make the FIRST line of your entry for this day?

We all got a little more burned today. We had a make-up lunch of su??? from scratch. It was pretty good.

I'm pretty sure that the word you're looking for here is "squid". If I recall correctly we got a can of the stuff in some kind of tomato sauce and a loaf of some quite tasty bread from the camp store.

We spent most of the day out in the sea and beach. We caught periwinkles and cooked some to eat.

A couple of quite vivid memories come rocketing back on this. I remember Dawn not wanting to dig in the sand for periwinkles because she was afraid she'd pull up a crab....which was *exactly* what happened after we finally convinced her to do it. Also, I remember me and you going up to the camp office with a full bucket of periwinkles to ask the guys there if we could eat them despite the fact that they couldn't

speak English (the camp staff, not the periwinkles) or us Spanish. I remember asking you what we would do if the periwinkles were protected or endangered or something like that and you suggested that we just take ONE periwinkle in, and if it was, indeed, illegal to catch them we could say, "Oh! Well, we'll just throw this one back then." I tell that story often and, oddly enough, no one seems to think it's as humorous as I do.

Also, frankly, if some stupid kids came up to me and asked me if they could eat some bottom-feeding mollusk they'd caught on my beach I would encourage them to do it regardless of if I knew they were edible or not. I am certain...CERTAIN...that they were watching us through binoculars while we were cooking and eating these things.

> *It was a very relaxing day and we plan to stay here another day and night. The price is right here at LA TORTUGA LIGERA.*
>
> *Well, here's to another day of ease.*

As I remember there was a bit of anxiousness regarding another camper and his radio.

Butch's Journal

Day 9 - June 9, 1982 - Barcelona, Spain

Our day of rest.

Because all the rest of the trip was just work, work, work.

You know, it really was a lot more work than it was a 'relaxing' sojourn. I wouldn't recommend our European tour to anyone looking for a casual jaunt through the old country...

Oh, quit yer bellyachin' you wimp…we were only a week into the trip and we're in the middle of four days on a Mediterranean beach! Tough life! But, really, you are quite correct, it was a physical effort. I would like to think I could do it again tomorrow, but I wonder sometimes.

Didn't do much except catch periwinkles, lie on the beach and listen to Fatty's music.

Fatty was one of the two guys camping near us (I doubt his name was actually "Fatty" but it was our cute little nickname for him....I can't remember why....). I never saw them do anything but lie in their tent and play their music. They could have been doing something productive like catching periwinkles or making fun of other campers.

I'd forgotten all about the tunes. It's probably what drove us to dive under water all day looking for food. And if I remember correctly…the water wasn't exactly azure blue.

Either that or we had never heard of salmonella.

> We cooked some periwinkles and Tony and Susi and I ate some. Dawn wouldn't get them near her mouth.

Obviously the smartest one of the bunch, and yet I made fun of her. I remember really trying to get her to eat one too. "C'mon Dawn, everybody's doing it. Just eat one. It's really cool."

I'd forgotten Dawn wouldn't eat the cute little buggers. Now it wasn't exactly Napoli's pizza, but they weren't that bad. I don't think Dawn would eat escargot at that little eatery by the Fasangarten S-Bahn stop, either.

The Foersterhaus…how could you forget that name? Yearbook staff dinners, prom committee dinners…that was a great place.

> Everyone else got sunburned today. Susi really bad, Dawn too, Tony not so bad.

Did this really happen or was it just wishful thinking on my sunburned part?

You were just wishing. I'll bet Dawn didn't get that burned either. You see, we'd spent a lot of time the summer before and later that summer on a beach in Lynn, Massachusetts working on our Spain pre-tan.

Oh yes, if there's one thing Massachusetts is known for it's the bronzed and buff beachgoers there. Second only to the English coast.

Of course now, I've got a map of melanomas on my body that science wants to study in depth (just kidding, Butch, don't get excited, I know you're looking for all of my capitalist maladies to put in your book).

Hey there Comrade, Capitalism is its own malady.

Tomorrow we're catching lots of winkles and cooking them for supper.

Living off the fat of the land I think was my objective here, misguided as it may be.

Boy, you were getting pretty familiar with our food, "winkles"? I was just hoping to get through the day without food poisoning symptoms.

Walked down to "Albatros" **(Susi's campground from the previous summer)** and it costs the same as here at "La Tortuga Ligera"

It meant "The Happy Turtle" didn't it?

There is a picture of a turtle on the postcard I have from here. He is smiling, you draw your own conclusion. My Spanish isn't that good.

Yes, but don't you think that the larger, textual question here is: WHY is the turtle smiling and does it mean he's really happy? If Willy Loman and Ishmael meant something larger, then might the turtle...oops...sorry...forgot where I was...

but it would be impractical to move.

Were we actually considering this? Or was I considering it to make my woman happy? At so many other points on this trip I was more

than willing to be impractical.

No, we talked about it. I think Susi still wanted to get back there. What really kept us from moving was about 100 ft. of rope with all of our wet wash still hanging on it. They would have loved us if they saw us coming with our clothes line in tow!

How nice of us to consider the management THERE and not the management at the place we were actually camping.

Tonight for supper we had squid and ravioli.

Because they're not just for breakfast anymore.

Mmmm. I'm betting Dawn went hungry again.

I'm not touching that bet.

That's the first time I had squid. After the periwinkles, squid was wimp food.

Not a good combo but it sure tasted good.

Which shows how hungry we really were....as if you needed more evidence after we ate the periwinkles.

Squid's still not bad. I get it sometimes in Chinatown in Boston.

But not as good as the sub we had for lunch.

Remember this sub? Man I sure do. It was huge, freshly baked bread and warm lunch meats and mayo....it doesn't get any better than that!

I didn't remember this until you brought it up. We bought everything at the little store, right? Even the mayo. I do remember that being a feast, now. Not bad. See, Spain wasn't that bad, up to this point.

Yep, bought it all right there. Now here's a question: we fixed the sub, we didn't have a cooler, it was summer in the Mediterranean, and, chances are we didn't use the whole jar of mayo (or, dear God, I hope we didn't) – What did we do with the jar of mayo? The various possibilities worry me.

Tomorrow is our last night here.

Or so we led Tony to believe.

And if it would have been, Spain would have been all right in my book!

I'm sure millions of Spaniards are sleeping well tonight knowing that.

NO MARGINAL NOTES OR POSTCARDS.

Tony's Journal

June 10, 1982

Today was a real lazy day. We were all too burned to sun any today so we slept, sat, and ate for the most part.

Still some of my favorite activities.

Mr. Bill and I did hunt for some periwinkles and we ate what we caught. I ate only a few though.

Meaning what here? That Mr. Bill ate A LOT?! I don't recall the periwinkle consumption being all that one sided.

You were always first in line…with my **Let's Go** ***book, by the way.***

Mr. Bill's burn got itchy and he was in agony for a while.

And people wonder why I don't like going to the beach.

Susi and Dawn played Mastermind while the "men" went periwinkling.

Recently came upon that travel edition of Mastermind (actually, it's the German version "SuperHirn Mini") while cleaning up. Had no idea that it made that trip with us...it's been through more than I thought.

We hope to leave early tomorrow morning to tour Barcelona and then leave that night for Madrid.

Ah, but such was not to be (he said in a needlessly ominous tone).

Butch's Barcelona postcards

Butch's Journal

Day 10 - June 10, 1982 - Barcelona, Spain

Another do-nothing day. My itching started up today, only on my chest, not my back.

Tony probably got a little excited here as it would have been the first mention of my rash in my own journal. As it was it was only the itching one gets from sunburn which, until that point, I had only gotten on my back and nowhere else. In the intervening years however I have managed to burn and itch all over my body. Have I mentioned that I love the sun and the beach?

I wasn't excited yet, but it was worth noting in my journal!

We just puttered around today. Cleaned out the tent, hunted periwinkles,

And we all know what clever prey they can be.

cooked 'em and ate 'em. Walked around. Nothing much.

As if you couldn't tell from the rest of the entry.

We tour Barcelona tomorrow and then leave for Madrid. The reason we didn't go out on the beach today was because everyone was so sunburned they couldn't take it.

MARGINAL NOTES: I have "Skol Cerveza" **in the margins again, guess we had some more of that and I've also got this rather cryptic note:** "So far: $85, DM10" **meaning up to that point, 10 days touring, and I'd spent just over $90 bucks. Gotta love those Southern European economies.**

The Orange Bible - Tony's "Let's Go" book...never out of Butch's hands.

Tony's Journal

June 11, 1982

Well, fate was against us last night. Our luck ran out and it rained. So, we couldn't leave for Madrid because our tents were too wet.

As I recall, that didn't stop us from leaving Monterosso the year before during spring break. Just ask the kindly Italian lady who had the misfortune to sit underneath your dripping backpack. And Od's Bodkins man, it RAINED…you make it sound like we lost our only shot window on a Moon mission or something. "Fate was against us…", "Our luck ran out…"

Instead we went into Barcelona and walked on the Ramblas. We made reservations for the 0820 train to Madrid. We ate a big lunch of Paella. It was pretty good. We are praying for clear skies tonight, but it doesn't look so good. Nevertheless, we'll have to go no matter. We went to Cataluna square and pigeons flew all over everybody. It was pretty fun.

Sure sounds exciting. I guess the novelty of it wears off after the seventh European city you're in and the pigeons do exactly the same thing.

I was disappointed that we didn't get to go today though. Oh well, that's life.

You know Tony....these entries are pretty short. Why do I have the feeling that you're leaving out all the really nasty shit you were saying about me? Don't hold back...well, actually, you can hold back on anything you have about my rash in London.......ah, what the hell, bring it on.

Paranoia will destroy you, my friend. I was a guy of few words.

Butch's Journal

Day 11 - June 11, 1982 - Barcelona, Spain

We went into Barcelona today finally.

What the hell was my hurry? I'd been here before.

We walked along the Ramblas to the train station where we mailed our postcards and made reservations for our train to Madrid. We ate at one of the restaurants in *Let's Go* called La Poste.

I seem to remember commenting on the synchronicity here as this was also the name of the place we used to go to all the time in Munich to eat mussels isn't it? (Well, ok, it was Zur Post and there's one in every German town but I remember someone commented on it).

We had paella. At least three of us had paella, Dawn hated it because it had seafood in it.

Dawn, I don't remember you being that high maintenance....of course, I didn't date you....Tony?

Some of the best seafood I've ever had in my life.

The periwinkles notwithstanding. What a fickle bastard I am.

I think the best meal we had on this trip was the last meal!

It was rice with some kind of spice (either saffron or curry) octopus, cuttlefish, squid, shrimp w/claws (crawdads?), short rib pieces, chicken, artichoke, eel, peas and mussels.

I wonder why it didn't occur to us that we were catching periwinkles by the handful and yet the little hole in the wall restaurant we went to didn't have them in their paella? Cheap, plentiful, and, apparently, *not* eaten by the locals.

On the coast paella has seafood but they make it all over the place in Spain with every area having its own kind. It always has rice and, although ours didn't, it most of the time has tomatoes.

Thank you Frugal Gormet. I wonder if I liked it...

We would have left today but it rained last night and our tents were wet and impossible to pack so we put it off a day.

Oh WOE is us! Whatever shall we DO? It RAINED! RAINED! So we must tarry here an extra DAY! Curse'd fates that hate us so, what could we have done to earn their enmity? Oh, alas…!

We're supposed to leave early tomorrow morning so we have to get up early. I think I'm getting that rash I got on the bike trip again.

The first mention of my rash. As you can see, I had it before on a bike trip I took back in '77 (another summer involving heavy packs, camping, hot weather, humidity, and sparse showers) so it wasn't new to me. Apparently, the only difference was that I told some folk this time much to the obvious delight of Mr. Savageau as it gave him something else to keep track of in his journal.

MARGINAL NOTES: I changed $20.00

POSTCARD: A very nice montage of Barcelona with an outline of Spain in the center and a soccer ball in the center of that. I wrote:

> #8
> June 11, 1982
> Rained - Sunburn these last 3 days - Leave tomorrow for Madrid
> - World Cup starts tomorrow.

Tony's Journal

June 12, 1982

Well, we got up at 0500 in the morning. No Rain. Hustled back in to Barcelona, and discovered, too late, that we were at the wrong train station in the city for the reservations we had. I am pretty mad.

That's funny, I don't remember anyone being "mad" per se. I remember feeling a little stupid.

My Spain 'sentence' was extended…that's all…I was bummed.

So we came to the central train station where our train leaves at 22:29. We are waiting now in the station and will have a 12 hr. wait, just for our train to leave. Then it is about a twelve hour train ride to Madrid.

If I remember correctly, we split up so one set of us could watch the bags at the train station, and the other couple could go do something. I can't for the life of me remember where you and Dawn went. I remember you leaving but don't recall where you went.

We haven't really eaten all that much today.

Maybe to get something to eat.

I think everyone is a little sick of Barcelona, so it was a let down when we found out we were at the wrong station. We sat out at the beach this morning for about 45 minutes watching the fishing trawlers. We are all very tired and a little on edge.

I don't remember that either. Time, being an excellent editor, has me remembering Barcelona as a great long break on our journey, hedonist campers living off the land and spending almost no money. Nowhere to be, nowhere to go (except the rest of Europe).

It will be good to get out of Barcelona. We have been here too long.

I guess you didn't feel that way.

Here's hoping we make it to Madrid.

Ahhh, the boundless optimism of youth! So refreshing in these cynical days of adulthood! Did you forget your meds or something?

No meds…just life experience. I'd lived a lifetime by the time I was 17…don't all 17 year olds??

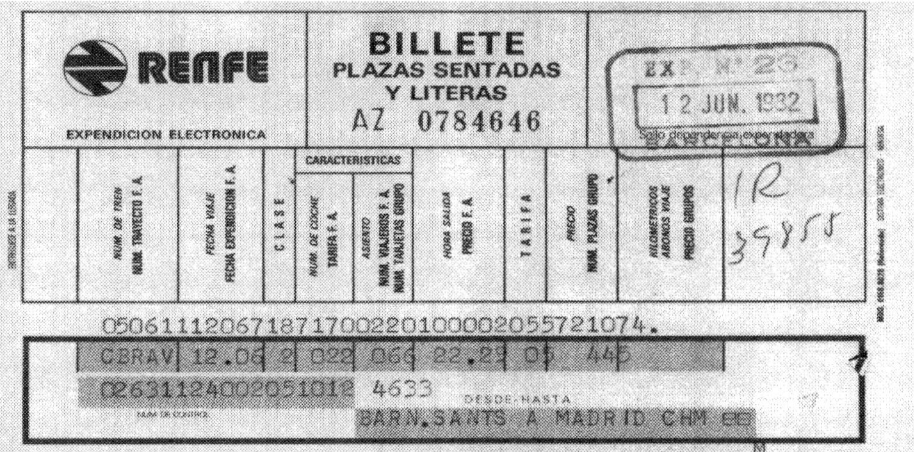

Butch's Journal

Day 12- June 12, 1982-Barcelona Spain

Missed our train so we made more reservations, went to the RIGHT train station and spent a lot of time there. Susi and I went across the street to a supermarket and bought some food then went to La Cathedral de la Sagrada Familia designed by Gaudi and climbed about halfway up.

I remember that building was one of the most incredible things I'd ever seen...and I remember killing time in that train station. Reading every English language thing we could get our hands on — the Simon and Garfunkel Concert in Central Park was the day before I remember the *Herald-Tribune* saying. And I remember Dawn and I trying to make a crank phone call to the most expensive hotel we could find and telling them we were some big millionaire and we wanted the whole 12th floor...after all these years it doesn't seem so funny....of course, now that I think about it, I don't recall it being so funny then.

I don't remember the crank call, y'all were the wild ones, I was a chicken!

Barcelona is strange; there are two people here: Spanish and Catalunyan. The Catalunyan language is almost like Spanish but older. The culture is older and there seems to be a surge of Catalunyanism within the last couple of years because when I was here two years ago I knew nothing about Catalunyanism. Also a big issue here now is the Mundial...the World Cup for Soccer. Everywhere you go you see something with the Orange Guy-the mascot- or the soccer ball leaving the Spanish flag as its trail or you see "Espana '82". This is on their money, stamps, postcards, etc. They seem to be going all out and capitalizing on it much the way the US did for the Bicentennial.

Now THERE'S a dated response.

It's interesting that your view centers on the culture and city while my views are mostly about sleep and food! (Still some of my top priorities by the way).

Perhaps...I wonder how much of what I wrote is actually correct...my Spanish wasn't very good so all of that must have been picked up randomly from observations I made while we were trotting through Barcelona and I was trying to talk you off the ledge.

But, unlike the US the Spanish have only one sport so when they get to have the World Cup it's an event we don't understand.

How utterly PC of me.

I do remember the World Cup stuff, I've got some pins from Scotland and England.

Tony's Journal

June 13, 1982

> *We got into Madrid pretty early in the morning. Surprisingly, I got a pretty good nite's sleep. We went to the geographical center of Spain and saw the Royal Palace as well. Because of the lousy train system, we have to go to Paris right away and pay a 400 pts ($4.00) supplement. That will be a 14 hour train ride. Dawn and I had BURGER KING for lunch in a park w/ Susi & Mr. Bill*

And we thought it was really nice of you guys to eat with us since you had so many other folks to choose from.

> *We played UNO also. We came back to the train station and I changed underwear, shirt, and socks for the first time since we first got to Spain.*

WHAT THE HELL?!?!? We did laundry in Barcelona! We were in Spain for four days!!! What were you waiting for?

France.

> *I almost lost my money pouch with everything in it when I changed, but I ran back and it was still there. (Thank God).*

That'll teach you not to change your underwear but once a week.

I'll be glad to get out of Spain.

Here we go.

This is the only place we have had any major setbacks.

"Major Setbacks"? It rained and we missed a train. Threw our highly detailed schedule off by one day. I think it's something personal.

Nope. Nothing personal. Loved Spain…just not as much of it as we were exposed to. Wanted to move on and see EUROPE, that's all.

Next we are off to Paris, but we are going to Chartres first, then back to Paris for a while. I hope things go smoother than here in Spain. So long for now.

I guess they didn't go smoother as I have no recollection of going to Chartres...and it's not in my journal....I've read ahead. Of course, with the speed we did Madrid and Paris, I suppose I could have missed it in there somewhere.

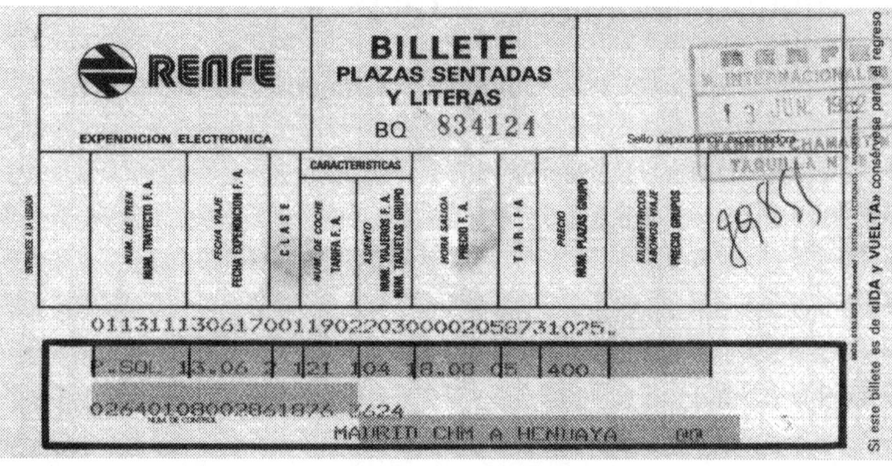

RENFE
EXPENDICION ELECTRONICA

BILLETE
PLAZAS SENTADAS
Y LITERAS
BQ 834124

Sello dependencia expendedora
INTERNACIONAL
13 JUN 1982
TAQUILLA N

NUM. DE TREN / NUM. TRAYECTO F.A. | FECHA VIAJE / FECHA EXPEDICION F.A. | CLASE | CARACTERISTICAS: NUM. DE COCHE / TARIFA F.A. | ASIENTO / NUM. VIAJEROS F.A. / NUM. TARJETAS GRUPO | HORA SALIDA / PRECIO F.A. | TARIFA | PRECIO / NUM. PLAZAS GRUPO | KILOMETROS / ABONOS VIAJE / PRECIO GRUPOS

9855

01131113061700119022030000205873 1025.

P.SOL 13.06 2 121 104 18.00 05 400

02640108002861876 3424

MADRID CHM A HENDAYA 00

Si este billete es de «IDA y VUELTA» consérvese para el regreso

Butch's Journal

Day 13-June 13, 1982-Madrid Spain

We got here about 09:30. We tried to find a train to Tours but no one knew anything about it. We supplemented

Sounds vaguely euphemistic and slightly illegal doesn't it?

and made reservations for a train to Paris.

Then we had to BUY a map of Madrid (40 ptas) to find out where to go to have a picnic. We took a metro to Puerta de Sol, the center of Madrid and of Spain, and from there walked down the Calle Mayor to try to find the Palacino Real (Royal Palace). We did find it I think. Then we headed back to the bahnhof

BAHNHOF? Pick a language and stick to it.

German still makes its way into my vocabulary almost every day.

to catch the 18:08 train to Paris.

I really regret not being specific enough here.

We met this Spaniard

In Spain, imagine…

named Roberto

In Spain, imagine…

who played Uno with us and shared his cognac with those in the car brave enough to try it. The guy sitting next to me didn't do much talking in English although he seemed to know a lot.

He looked like Guy Cabellero on SCTV (Why, yes, I did watch a lot of TV, why do you ask?).

I remember thinking our Spanish friend might be a Basque terrorist.

Because you always look on the bright side of every situation.

I try to see all sides…that's all. I don't get to him until tomorrow in my journal. I do remember the SCTV likeness now though!

The whole car got to talking like a "family." We changed trains at 02:00 and I got to stretch out for about 2 hours before some people came in.

Tony's Journal

June 14, 1982

Our train ride was pretty good all in all. We had a Spanish dude who shared his Brandy (he called it Congac)

And I'm inclined to believe him.

with us and played UNO. When we got to the Spanish/French boarder, we stayed in a train car we could stretch out and sleep till Paris. Got to Paris and it took us about 2.5 hours to find a hotel from the train station w/ rooms. We found one about a mile or so from the station, if even that far, called the "Café Hotel les Facultes", 5 rue Linne. It's pretty cheap. The four of us are staying in one room for FF96.50 ($16.00) and it's in the Latin Quarter and surprisingly quite adequate with a sink and bathroom down the hall. We are on the fourth floor.

That place is so vivid in my memory I think due to the fact that we hadn't seen a bed in over a week. The bedspreads, the little (and I seem to remember REALLY little) balcony over the street...(in fact, now that I'm thinking about it a bit more, it could have been just two big windows), the fourth floor with our packs...very vivid.

After we got settled here, we walked through the Place de la Contrescarpe to the Notre Dame cathedral. We ate across from it too.

Oh so! I see who was much more specific with the meal in this particular case.

We then took a metro to the "L'Arc de Triomphe." We could see the Eiffel Tower in the distance. We walked down the entire Champs Elyssees to the Cleopatra Needle. We took our time and stopped at a few places on the way, so we got to see the Arc lit up. We are going tomorrow to most of these places again because we got to the sights as most were closing up. We also walked by the Grand & Petit Palais.

I think one of us was copying out of the other's journal. Our entries are remarkably the same.

The Louvre will be closed, so unfortunately we won't be able to see the paintings & other art there. This place is rather expensive, but I like it a lot. I got all of my languages mixed up and I have my "Eau de..." Too bad we couldn't afford another day here.

I don't remember, were we leaving because of money or time? I remember we left London early because we were hemorrhaging money, but I don't recall that being the reason we left Paris. It's a good thing we did, however, because of that rail strike in the UK a week and a half later. If we had stayed in Paris another day we would have been stuck in the UK during the strike instead of getting out by the skin of our teeth.

Well, have to enjoy it while I can. Maybe we'll try a little wash again at a Laundromat. That should be something.

Yes, because, apparently, you only brought 2 pair of underwear and socks.

Butch's Journal

Day 14-June 14, 1982-Paris, France

Spent about 2 hours in the train station

What...not Bahnhof?

from 10:30-12:30) trying to find a place to stay. We finally found a place right near the station that cost 96.50ff for four people. That comes to about 24ff per person, the place is called Cafe Hotel les Facultes

Just a tad better than the train we slept on the night before.

and it's in, supposedly, the best part of the Latin Quarter on the Left Bank of the Seine. It's close to the Louvre and Notre Dame.

We were pretty much in synch here based on journal entries.

We ate at a cafeteria after searching the Contrescarpe for a cheap place to eat. My dinner of French fries, steak, bread, and watermelon w/Perrier was only about 26ff. Not bad. Then we took half the tour of Notre Dame, the tower where Quasimodo did his stuff was closed because it was too late. Then we took the metro to the Arc de Triomphe and walked down the Champ Elysees taking side trips to look at the Grand Palais and the Petit Palais and the Eiffle Tower from the Seine.

Now I have a recollection that at some point in Paris we ate at a Burger King on the Champ, although I didn't record that significant event. This girl I dated, after Dawn dumped me in college, was in Paris (we found out later) the same days we were and ate at that Burger King too. I'll have another weird encounter to tell you about when we get to Dublin later in June.

We didn't eat there...too pricey and they didn't have periwinkles on the menu...we only went in...one by one...to use the bathroom.

> We walked down to Cleopatra's Needle and saw the Arc lit up. We were gonna walk the gardens of the Louvre but they closed it up so we took the metro to a stop 2 minutes away from our hotel. Tomorrow night we either leave for either London or Dublin after seeing the rest of Paris.

Because, you know, we don't want to stay in Paris too long, after wasting those 10 hours in Madrid we don't want to be hanging around Paris for more than 24...36 hours...we've got things to do. We should market our route. "How to see Paris in less than Two Days." We'd make a fortune.

Whenever I think back on our trip, I still look at Paris as being the one big European city we visited that I really enjoyed. You'll see more on that in tomorrow's entry. If it weren't so expensive, I would have liked to hang out there rather than rainy old Spain (you must remember that my fore-fathers were hanging out in France during the Crusades, so it's in my blood!).

"Rainy old Spain"??!?!?
ONE NIGHT! It rained ONE NIGHT!

Marginal Notes: Apparently, while we were there they devalued the currency so we made out great. I have this marginal note concerning that:

Dollars to French Francs
Before Devaluation:
$1 = 6.05ff

After Devaluation:
$1 = 6.57ff

I changed $20

Post card: The postcard I have for this stop was never sent (I guess we were in and out of Paris so fast we didn't have time to stop at a post office). It's just a normal Paris postcard with a picture of the Tower on one half and Notre Dame on the other.

You know, I picked up this habit of sending myself a postcard from places I've been just to record the event. What an impression you made on me!

Tony's Journal

June 15, 1982

Butch and I were the first up, so we went to an automatic laundry and did some wash.

What liberated guys we were. Letting the womenfolk sleep while we went off to wash our unmentionables. I seem to remember Susi and Dawn were always the last to awaken....is that right?

We left around noon to find out how to get to the UK. We had to pay a 69FF ($11) to get across the Channel. We have to go to London first. Anyway, we left the station and spent a lot of time looking for a place to eat. We decided on a small café. Dawn and I had Ham & Cheese omelets at 47.60FF ($8) for the both of us. I have spent $50 in two days on mostly food. That was about the only meal we had today. After we ate, we walked to the Eiffel Tower where Dawn and I went up to the top (about 998 ft) for 26FF ($4.25) each.

Money is starting to become a real concern all around it looks like. I mention it a little more in my journal too. If you recall I ran out and had to call my mom to wire some in Ireland...but I'm jumping ahead a bit in the tale. Susi and I didn't go up to the top of the Tower with you guys because of the money thing. In fact, now that I'm thinking (even more) about it, the "rich dudes" we met who were cruising around Europe in rented cars we met while you and Dawn were in the Tower.

I think it was worth it because you could see everything of importance within the city from there.

Oh sure, rub my nose in it.

I had a lot of fun here and I think the city is very cool, although expensive. Now we are off to London, which is about 10 hrs. away. Almost forgot, all had excellent night's sleep and I have been bothered the last two days w/ shin splints and Dawn has a swollen knee & Butch some "jock itch".

OOOOOOOokay, here we go! Tony's obsession with my rash begins! And the quote marks are a nice touch. Draw your own conclusions. ("jock itch" yeah, right, because I was such a jock) Ahhhh yes, the rash. Oh, the joys of summer travel in less than ideally hygienic environments.

It's not an obsession yet. Just an observation. But it's building.

Other than those small inconveniences, everything is great.

Butch's Journal

Day 15- June 15, 1982- Paris, France

After waking up from a great night's sleep in a real bed Tony and I went to wash clothes. After doing that we checked out and went to the train station to see about ferry fares, reservations, etc. We had to change our plans because from LeHavre to Ireland is too expensive we'll be taking the 22:35 "Midnite Ferry" train to London. Today we did a lot of walking and looking for a restaurant that was listed in Let's Go.

I do remember this quite well. As I recall, tempers were getting A LITTLE short as we were walking and walking and walking, couldn't find it and we were all REALLY hungry.

I remember this well too. I remember walking all over the place, book in hand and we found ourselves in the middle of a new apartment or office park saying, yep this is the place...

We never found it so we walked some more until we found a cafe where we all had omelets. Real, French omelets. Good stuff. Then we went to the Eiffel Tower and walked around. It's impressive.

Pretty stingy with the adjectives for something like the Eiffel Tower huh?

Yeah, did you guys go to the top with us? I think you did, but I didn't mention it in my journal nor did you. I know funds were

starting to be an issue with everyone...except money bags Dawn (it's nice to be the only child isn't it?).

We met this rich dude from Queens, New York who was renting a car around Europe. Never caught his name. Then we walked a little more on the Champ Elysees, took a metro to the Louvre and walked in the garden there. Then went to the station to catch our train. Paris was fun, a little expensive,

You know, it probably wasn't all that expensive, we MIGHT have been spoiled from paying $2.50 a night in Spain.

Nah, I remember the expense side too. Note in my journal I was concerned that I'd spent $50 already or about 15% of my total spending money for the trip.

but fun because we finally toured a city, for the most part, on foot

BOY DID WE EVER!

You know, in my photo album, I have pictures of us at the after prom party in Venice and then the pics from throughout the trip. With all the walking and one meal a day plan, it looks like I dropped about 15-20 lbs. over the month! I was probably never in as good a shape as I was after our trip!

which is a great way to see all the city has to offer. It would have been nice to walk around a bit more but I'm satisfied. The Parisians aren't nearly as arrogant as I thought

Oh, very nice! I'm sure the Parisians were just thrilled by my seventeen-year-old pearls of wisdom! What the hell?!?!?!

they would be and much more tolerant of tourists than regular Frenchmen.

Basing that on WHAT I have no idea as I don't think I'd ever been to another part of France other than the Riviera cities and I don't remember thinking those folk were particularly intolerant. I apologize to the French for perpetuating the stereotype...although, really, I seem to be saying that the stereotype is wrong don't you think?

I was very impressed with the city as a whole. It's what I expected and not what I expected.

I wish I could have been a little more vague here.

Very Nice. London Next.

Kontrolle	Datum	Von	nach
	15.06.82	PARIS	LONDON
		über DUNKERQUE	DOVER
	17.06.82	LONDON	Salisbury
		über	
	19/20.06.82	Salisbury	INVERNESS
		über LONDON	
	22.06.82	INVERNESS	GIASGOW
		über	
	22/23.06.82	GIASGOW	BELFAST
		über STRANRAER	LARNE

Tony's InterRail pass book - third leg

Tony's Journal

June 16, 1982

The train ride and two hour Channel crossing weren't so bad. We got to Victoria Station in London early in the morning and were checked into a youth hostel on Carner Lane just down from Fleet Street and St. Paul's church. We roamed around London and bought a London Rover Pass for the Tubes.

We were soooooo very continental. We both used "tubes" in our journal like it was the world we always used for the subway. Which, now that I think about it, was "s-bahn" since we lived on them in Munich. Perhaps we WERE very continental.

We went to Mme. Tausauds, the Planetarium, both on Baker Street. We then went to see the Houses of parliament and Westminster Abbey. We took a double-decker bus from there to Trafalgar Square where we fed the pigeons and they graced us with what they are famous for.

Unlike, as I recall, the Spanish pigeons who were quite tidy.

After we ate we walked around and saw the Sherlock Holmes Pub then we went to see the Laser show. After that, we went to the Piccadilly Circus for ole time's sake and walked around till about 9:45pm.

Actually, until you said "for old time's sake" I had totally forgotten our previous trip to London 19 months earlier. You, me and Mike walking through Piccadilly singing Beatles songs at the top of our lungs (sober yet!) so overwhelmed were we with that British spirit. I think we missed a very good opportunity to get the shit kicked out of us.

We came back to the hostel and slept. Butch's "rash" is getting worse too.

You know, you seem a bit too interested in my rash. I was in agony. I'm glad it provided you with something to write about. However, putting quotation marks around it gives it a rather euphemistic air that I'm not sure I like. Kind of like, you know, she was "sick" or, Bob and Joe are good "friends." It was a damn rash and it was annoying as hell!

It seems we saw a lot of things, but then when I think back to last time I was here, we are gonna miss a number of interesting sights that are impossible to cover in a day and a half and keep within our expense accounts. Butch is already down to $80, I have $160 left, Susi probably a little more, and Dawn is living easy with about $500 left.

Huh...Butch broke...imagine. Did I say something earlier about the more things changing...?

We hope to get to Salisbury and Stonehenge tomorrow and then go up north. We hope, that is, before we run out of money.

Which I soon did.

FREE
WELCOME TO LONDON
Tourist Information, Underground and Bus Maps
1982

Butch's Journal

Day 16-June 16, 1982- London, England

We found a room after we got to Victoria Station right off the bat at a youth hostel for 3.75 pounds per person. Nice and big.

"Nice and Big" what the hell was I saying? Of course it was nice and big, it was a goddam barracks. There were about a hundred beds in there. "Nice and Big" Sheesh.

I do remember the barracks like feel. It seems the bathroom was a long way away.

There was a bathroom in that place?

Little did we know what a real barracks was like until we hit Dublin later in the month.

Then we explored London, my third time. We got a tube pass and, for breakfast, went to Dunkin' Donuts

Can you tell we were living in Europe for the last few years? This trip has been a succession of KFC's, Burger Kings, Dunkin' Donuts. THESE were the foreign restaurants to us.

I think we were just getting jazzed up to go back to the good old U. S. of A.! You can't just re-immerse yourself into the native culture you know.

then to Baker Street, THE Baker Street,

I really don't know why I was so impressed with Baker Street. I may have read a Sherlock Holmes short story at some point prior to this, but it was over a decade later before I really got into Holmes stories. This would (should?) mean a lot more to me now than then. I'm stumped. Perhaps I liked the idea of this place they set up (at 221B Baker St.) to be Holmes' residence when he was, in fact, a fictional character. Who knows.

My Baker Street recollection was from the song! You can see that my cultural exposure didn't get much beyond Kasey Kasem and the top 40 countdown.

I always wondered why you seemed so light in your head and dead on your feet that day.

and toured Madame Tussauds Wax Museum and the Planetarium. Then we went to see the Houses of Parliament, Westminster Abbey and Big Ben. From there we went to Trafalgar Square and fed the pigeons.

What...AGAIN?

So, we were bird lovers, what do you want? Wasn't it right across from the square you got your cream for the "nappy rash"? It happens all the time in the London, the guy knew just what the Yank needed to clear things up! I didn't record the phrase near as I can tell, but not a week goes by that the "nappy rash" doesn't work its way into my lexicon. Now the rash observation was becoming a hot topic of conversation in my tent!

Once again, you not only bring up the rash, you know where I got the cream! I had actually forgotten "nappy rash" and I doubt I would

have known what it meant at the time but "nappies" are diapers...I just read that the other day. So there, you can put quotes around it all you like, all I had was a bad case of very adult and masculine diaper rash.

By the way, that can of cream (more of a WAX actually) hung around every medicine cabinet I had for about six or seven years...and I don't recall ever using it again.

We ate in a little cafe right across from the square.

I remember chicken. A big plate of roasted chicken. That's all I remember about the place.

Sure, you* REMEMBER *chicken, but you couldn't afford it pal. You and I settled for good old English pizza, just like mama used to make. Dawn (with all the money) had the nice plate of chicken. I think we may have just been drooling or at least plotting ways to separate Dawn from her money pouch.

Hey, I know I had a piece of chicken. Probably while Dawn was in the bathroom or something. Ahhhh, English pizza.

After that we made our way back to Madame Tussaud's to see the laser show. Coolest thing I've ever seen.

Oh yeah, MUCH cooler, I'm sure, than that old Eiffel Tower, or the Leaning Tower, or the Colosseum, or the Vatican, or Big Ben or anything else we saw JUST ON THIS TRIP!

Now come on, the coolest thing on the trip? I think the birds crapping on our heads was much more exciting.

Worse! Look at what I said! I said it was the "coolest thing I've EVER seen." If I said that out loud during the trip I hope one of you

reached over and slapped me silly!

I wouldn't have slapped you. All the crying you were doing about your nappy rash and sun burn was enough for all of us.

After that it was dark so we went to Piccadilly Square and wandered around.

Which, you know, is exactly the right time for four 17 year olds to go to wandering around Piccadilly. So much more dangerous than in the daytime, it's a good thing we waited.

Butch, think about the whole trip and the places we stayed, slept, ate and walked around with that invincibility of youth. Piccadilly was a cake walk. We were just getting ready for the Irish to threaten to blow up our train and throw rocks at us.

Actually, I'm much more impressed with our survival skills 15 months earlier when we were camping in Italy. "Oh, sure, we can sleep right here in the train station. See, that guy is doing it…wonder why he chose that puddle to sleep in…"

Then made our way back to the hostel.

You know, we did a hell of a lot for one day in London!

I'm telling you! We had a plan: never stay more than 36 hours in one place. We saw Paris in the time most people tour Graceland. I'm guessing we missed a few things though…

Marginal Notes: According to my marginal notes the address of that hostel was 36 Carter Lane. **Also,** I changed $20 and 100ff. **The exchange rate that day was** 1 pound = $1.79.

POSTCARD: Once again, a nice montage of London sights. Big Ben, Houses of parliament, St. Paul's, Piccadilly Circus, Trafalgar Square, I'm sure no one ever got such a nice postcard of London. The stamp is a really nice one of Lord Nelson and the HMS Victory which I remember picking out specifically at the post office. The notes on the postcard are:

> #11 June 16, 1982
> EXPENSIVE LONDON – DUNKIN DONUTS – WIMPYS – MADAM TUSSAUDS – LASARIUM TONITE – GONNA GET OUT OF HERE TOMORROW

Tony's Journal

June 17, 1982

We got up and left the hostel pretty early and went to Dunkin Donuts for something to eat. We then walked to the Waterloo station. Found out that the sector we stayed in, Blackfriars, was the old stomping grounds of William Shakespeare.

I have no memory of knowing that. Thanks.

After checking our backpacks, we walked to Buckingham palace and were in time to see part of the changing of the guards. The four of us also got to sign the Queen's guest book, which she looks at every two weeks.

Check out Tony with the extra details.

From there we walked to Hyde Park and sat for a little while. We did some shopping for food and then we were back to the station to catch a train to Salisbury. Salisbury has an old gothic church,

That church, which has the highest spire in the UK and one of the oldest by the way, has been revisited upon me time and time again in my Renaissance class, my art history class, and my History of Religion class. One of the professors even had photos of the INSIDE of the spire that he took when he climbed up in there one summer. The way they would construct these things back in the 1200's is that

they would build this huge wheel up in the spire and use it as a pulley to lower and raise supplies and people. When they were finished they would chop up the wheel and throw it down because, well, it was the 1200's...wood was valuable. HOWEVER, this is one of the few churches in all of Christendom in which the wheel was left in the spire....and it's still there today. Thought you might like to know what an unusual church it is.

but the real reason we came here was to see Stonehenge about 10 mi. away. We are camping in a youth hostel for Pound 1.30 per person. Not bad. We walked down to an old English pub and had some ale. Came back to go to sleep but some locals pulled up a stake and maybe cut the rope to part of Butch's tent.

ACTUALLY, just for the sake of accuracy, I believe it was Mark Hooper's tent, not 100% sure about that, but I know it wasn't mine.

Well, tomorrow we bike to Stonehenge.

....against the deluge.

Butch's Journal

Day 17 - June 17, 1982 - London-Salisbury, England

We woke up, checked out, went to Dunkin Donuts and Waterloo Station where we dropped our stuff off. Then we walked to Buckingham palace via St. James Park. At the palace we saw the changing of the guards, or at least the last half, and we signed the Queen's guest book.

I remember this well. We thought we would get to go inside the palace like they used to do and instead the guard took us to this little dinky guard house and we got to sign some spiral bound notebook. (Ok...maybe it wasn't a spiral bound notebook but it wasn't the gilt-edged, leather-bound, vellum-paged tome you had to sign with a quill that I was expecting).

I know. I remember thinking how impressive it was going to be that the Queen would see our names. But when they said she '"looked" at the book once every two weeks, she probably leaned out a window and the guard waved it at her from the hut. There, she looked at it again!

Then we walked through Hyde Park for awhile, went to a supermarket for supper

Probably because we were tired of all that rich food we'd been eating and wanted something simple. One can only take so much pizza and Dunkin Donuts.

> and walked back to Waterloo Station to catch our train to Salisbury. We left at 16:38 and arrived at 18:05. Hiked to the youth hostel - Milford Hill House - where we got a special rate because we camped in the back. Then we went to a real English pub, Odd Fellows Arms, and had some real English ale approved by CAMRA (the Campaign for Real Ale).

I remember this really impressing me, but I can't for the life of me remember why. I can tell how excited I was because the entry has me just talking about the ale and the pub and not mentioning the fact that the four of us sat a table for an hour and no one ever spoke to us.

I remember the ale, but not the atmosphere all that much.

> We got back about 22:00 and went to sleep. At about 23:15 we were awakened by someone looking for "Joan." As they were leaving they broke our tent string and pulled a stake out. They came back about 15 minutes later and banged on Tony's tent. I got out and asked them about our tent rope. They said it was a friend of theirs who "talks exactly like me." I stayed out waiting for them to leave but they stayed.

I remember you getting mad at me about this because while I was waiting for them to leave I was talking to them. I was hungry to talk to some locals and everyone ignored us at the pub. I hope you put something in your journal about it. I remember being mad at you because I was afraid of these drunk guys and wanted you to come out too. I knew I would get back in the tent and then their friend who "talks exactly like me" would come back and cut the rest of our tent ropes.

Well, as you saw, my journal entry recorded this in a single sentence. But I do remember it well. Dawn and I awoke and heard you guys talking. I was going to go out and see what was up, but Dawn wanted to sit tight and listen. I do remember saying something like, "Where's my knife (or gun?)", trying to intimidate them from within. I remember thinking if they started a fight, I'd have to go out no matter what Dawn was saying (was I that whipped?).

The first time the lady yelled they didn't do anything but the second time they yelled back at her and ran. We got in our tent, with the cat,

I can't remember; did you guys bring a cat too or just us? Nothing like bringing a cat on a train trip around Europe....really adds to the experience.

You've got me on that one. I don't remember a cat, and I don't really remember anyone yelling out at us. I do remember them wanting to kick us out the next day because they thought we were cause of the commotion. I also remember this was the first time I'd ever had tea with milk in it.

Actually, I have very little recollection of the cat, seems like he belonged to the hostel and they let him have free reign.

and went to sleep.

Tony's Journal

June 18, 1982

> *It poured last night and some of our stuff got a little bit wet. We rented four bikes and biked the ten miles to Stonehenge in the pouring rain. We were soaked to the bone. It was very interesting considering it was four thousand years old. By the time Dawn and I had burned our mouths off on some of the hottest mustard I ever tasted, and we just sat around talking, we were pretty dry.*

One sentence on Stonehenge, right to the weenies.

It's not every day you get a good English hot dog. Stonehenge's are a dime a dozen. I think there's even one up in New Hampshire — Salem I think.

> *So, we set off for the return journey. It was a good bike ride back because it didn't rain on the way back. We fed some ducks and took a few pictures.*

These must have been some pretty impressive ducks to make both journals.

I remember sheep as well, but they didn't make the journal.

> *Because we took it leisurely, it took about two hours. That's*

> *not a bad time considering conditions. Mr. Bill's rash is getting better.*

Well praise the lord and pass the nappy rash ointment! At last something positive about my rash. You know, it has raised its ugly head ONCE in my journal, but yours seems to have been covering it for both of us.

It was a nightly topic in our tent. I almost went into medicine because of you and Susi.

> *Hope it doesn't rain again 'cause we want to leave tomorrow night. It looks OK now. The lady who 'runs' the place was mad at us because she thought it was our fault for all the noise the locals were causing last night messing with the tents.*

Yeah, well, I set her straight. She didn't mess with us again.

> *Dawn says she's not having a good time. I don't know if she's serious or not though.*

So, 15 years later and the truth comes out. Actually, no big secret here, I remember a little farther along in the trip, when it was winding down I mentioned something about how I'd like to start all over and do it again. I remember Dawn stuck in a quick, "Not Me!" So I kinda figured she wasn't having the best of times. Any idea why? Dawn, you MIGHT be able to shed some light on this.

I think it was the mustard, that's what opened it up...

> *I'm surprised the four of us have not had any bad scenes yet.*

There's one a-brewing however. I seem to remember a bit of a blow up surrounding County Cork, hitch-hiking, and tickets to see The Pirates of Penzance. I haven't read ahead in my journal so I don't

know if I make any mention of it. I hope you did as I never knew how mad you really were.

I haven't read ahead that far yet either. I think the Cork thing was a combo of factors, the impending rail strike, kissing the Blarney stone, bus schedules back to see the show, losing the camera, then finding it. I don't think I ever get mad per se, just overly worried, you know? I'm not going to read ahead, but that Cork stuff will all come out in a week or so...

> *Tomorrow we plan to head off to Scotland after doing a little wash first. That's about all to say for now I guess.*

You know, I was thinking back to the week or so we were in the UK and it was pretty historic time. The Falkland War ended the first or second day we were there. Prince William was born around then. Alexander Haig resigned after all the flak he took for 'being in charge' when Reagan was shot earlier. And, of course the rail strike, which we'll be getting to. All we needed was a Nessie sighting and we would have been golden!

Tony, Butch, Susi - the Salisbury Deluge Bike Trip

Butch's Journal

Day 18 - June 18, 1982 - Salisbury, England

The first thing worth mentioning that happened was the lady telling us that she didn't want us here. I explained to her that it wasn't us but the two English guys.

Boy, that's a clear couple of sentences. Let's see if I can translate: Early this morning the woman ("lady"...sheesh...who am I? Jerry Lewis?) at the front desk told us that she didn't want us staying the extra night I had requested due to the shenanigans the previous night. I related to her the story of the two hooligans who had accosted us in our tents during the night in question. Two males, apparently of English decent. (Which I'm sure was real unusual there in the heart of England. Constables picked them up almost immediately no doubt. "Good thing you recognized their accents as English, Old Bean," they said, "really helped us crack this case. Good show and all that rot. Cheerio.")

Butch, it was due to your sweet talking abilities that kept us in the back yard. I remember them wanting to kick us out the next day but you had a good story!

And I was still a week away from kissing the Blarney Stone.

She said that if ever we had trouble again to ring at the side door and let us stay. After Susi and I got back from changing money we all rented a bike.

I'm going to make a leap here and say that what I actually meant was that we all rented DIFFERENT bikes, or, rather, a bike apiece.

I think you're right...the pictures confirm it.

Then we went back to the bank for Dawn to change money and Susi and I went to the market. By then it was pouring down raining and we had had hopes of pedaling to Stonehenge, 10 miles up the road. When it lightened up some (not much) we set out. My red sweatshirt ran red like crazy, on my pants, hat,

Hat? I had a hat? On my round head? I must have looked like Frosty. Anyone have a photo of me in my lid?

Yeah, I've got about four pics of the Stonehenge trip. I do see your red sweatshirt, but I'm the only one in a hat, at least in these pics. We look like drowned rats! Now, I do have a picture of us at Trafalgar square and you've got this white Gillgan's Island hat on there. I guess that's why the pigeons didn't really bother you that much.

shirt, hands and body. Stained big time.

I had the underwear from that trip for a couple years after that and the red from my brand new sweatshirt never came out of them. Which sort of surprised me as all it took was rain to make it leave the sweatshirt and yet 3 years of washing it didn't get it out of the underwear. (I could understand if it was Tony's underwear as he only washes his underwear once or twice a year.)

I was just trying to be environmentally conscious, way before my time.

By the time we got there we were soaked, cold and a little tired and it was still raining a bit. We saw Stonehenge (60p). Impressive. Not much really but eerie. And awesome to think that they have been there for 4000 years.

THAT'S IT? That's all I say about one of the great mysteries of the ancient world? How about the way the plain looked as the sun was breaking through the rain clouds? How about the fact that it was only a day or two away from the Summer Solstice and Salisbury Plain was slowly filling up with druids and hippies? I remember all this shit, why didn't I write any of it down???? I guess I wanted to hurry up and get to the part about the hot dogs...because that was the important stuff.

The sun started coming out and the wind blowing, we started drying out, feeling a little better so we ate lunch. Dawn and Tony had hot dogs with this mustard that looked like regular but was 99 44/100% horseradish. It was funny.

Because it wasn't me.

This is probably the most vivid memory for me at Stonehenge too. Forget the relics, they'll be there in another four thousand years, but that mustard! I remember getting my hot dog and slopping the mustard on with this tiny little spoon. I remember thinking, what's up with this little spoon? One bite, my head was clear for a week after that. To this day, I can't eat horseradish!

We were almost dry when we left. The sun was shining and it was even a little warm. On the way back we stopped and fed some ducks.

Two sentences about Stonehenge but I get the hot dogs and ducks in.

As soon as we got into town we went to the train station to check times, then went back to the hostel. Our tents weren't even damp. We took our showers (soooooo nice). Even had my own shampoo. Shaved, the works.

I read that last line a couple of times in my journal before I saw the comma. The pen skipped apparently. I had no memory of having "shaved the works" and was glad I cleared that up.

Went inside to catch up on this (the journal) and watched a little World Cup on the TV. Then we went downtown to get some fish 'n' chips.

Postcard: Didn't mail it but it's all addressed and ready to go. It's got a nice picture of Stonehenge on the front (with a sky much bluer than the one we were under) and on the back I wrote:

#12, June 18, 1982
Rode 10 miles on rented bikes to see Stonehenge in the rain - pretty countryside coming back - having a great time.

And I meant it too.

Well, that made one of you. (See my journal)...

Dawn, Susi, Butch - the trip home - a bit less moist

Tony's Journal

June 19,1982

We were woken up by the lady who runs the hostel, so we packed up our stuff and stored them so we could explore Salisbury on foot. We walked to a super market first and got a little something for breakfast.

What? You didn't record what we had for breakfast?

After that, we made our way to the public library where we sat around and read for two hours. Dawn called her mom from there and talked for about two minutes. From the library we walked across the street to the market and I bought some green gooseberries. They were pretty good, but not as sour as I remembered.

I have no memory of this. What was the deal with the gooseberries? Were you pressuring us to try gooseberries?

No, I don't think so. I'd just not seen any since the few summers I spent in North Dakota.

Then we walked through a few of the stores that were open before going to the Cathedral. The Cathedral has England's highest spire and they were celebrating mass at the time we walked in so we sat out on the lawn.

First you get kicked out of the Vatican and then we go barging in on some mass. We were some irreverent little heathens on this trip.

From there we walked back to the hostel where Dawn & I had peanut butter and jelly sandwiches.

But Tony, what did Susi and I have?

(Why does this next line sound like a Cousteau documentary?)

From the hostel we said goodbye to Salisbury and the land of Hardy and of Stonehenge and

...the crew of the Calypso...

set out for London to catch a connecting train at 21:45 for Inverness, Scotland. Right now we are waiting for the train to leave. Susi and Dawn have come down with the sniffles because of yesterday's bike ride.

Yet another reason for Dawn to enjoy her European trek.

We bought two brain teaser puzzle booklets to keep us busy on the longer trips.

Did we ever crack either one of them? I doubt our brains were working too well by this point in the trip.

The one tonight will be about 13 hrs. We didn't do any wash after all because of "a serious lack of funds". As of today:

Me	*Dawn*	*Butch*	*Susi*
$120	*$280*	*$70*	*$140*

I really want to get to Ireland and so does Dawn, for her parent's sake. She says her dad is excited about it. Well, we have a nice big compartment to the four of us and I'm gonna get some shut eye.

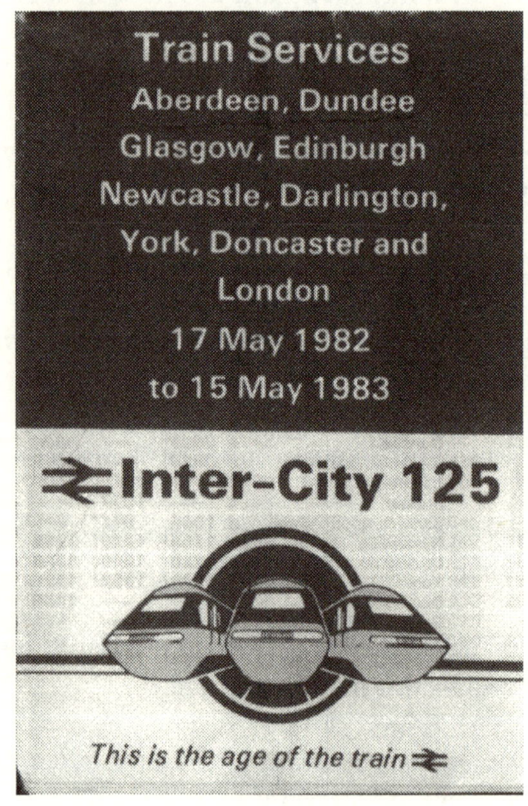

Butch's Journal

Day 19 - June 19, 1982 - Salisbury, England

Today we checked out of the hostel - left our packs there though – and walked around. We went to the library, the market and the cathedral

I remember this day very well. I thought it very relaxing especially after the previous day's adventures. I remember we spent some time in the public library looking at books about America and the English take on it. I remember this one book we looked at was about how to survive a vacation to America and it gave little tips on what to do and say and how to buy stuff and how to pronounce certain English words (the word "fillet," for example. I recall that it said that Americans have the need to pronounce it as a French word. It's pronounced as it's spelled in England and if pronounced that way in American the customer would not get what he ordered.) I also recall that it was a beautiful day, quite different than the weather the day before (of course, that could just be my memory playing tricks on me as I don't record it....hell, we could have spent all that time in the library to get out of the rain....but I don't think so).

Even though I wrote about the library too, I don't remember all that much about it. I remember the Open Market and walking around, seeing the cathedral. However, you told me more about the cathedral the other day than I recall getting from you then! See Butch's comments below.

Yeah, I got more out of the trip the older I got and went back and learned about the stuff I actually saw. We seem to have made a point to see stuff other people said would be important to see regardless of if we had heard of it or not. It seems to have worked out however.

- the cathedral has the highest spire in the British Isles and it's one of the oldest built in 1220. It's really impressive.

No comments here from me thankfully. I dealt with this a couple of days ago ad nauseum.

We did a little shopping then came back to the hostel to pick up our stuff and eat. We decided we'd go to Loch Ness

We only decided this then? I found a map of our trip as it finally turned out, but I don't have a copy of that map we made BEFORE our trip. How our trip was GOING to be. Does anyone else?

I've got the whole trip (pictures, journal, ticket stubs, maps, etc.) in this old green photo album (or alblum as I used to say) with that one sticky side and the see through pages. Anyway, the old thing has adhered like cement. When I pried my journal from it clutches, I practically lost the back cover page. I have an interail map, I tried to get it out the first day we started all this, but it started to tear. I'm going to have to find a way to pry it out, because I think it's what you're looking for.

Yeah, those things are deadly. Try a blowdryer to loosen up the cement and then rubbing alcohol to get the glue off the items (and the blow dryer, and your fingers, and the dining room table you're working on, and then some lacquer to replace the finish on the table that the rubbing alcohol took off...)

but to do that we have to go back to London

Which, we learned, you have to do to go anywhere in England from anywhere else in England

so we caught the 18:20 train to London and from there took the metro to the right station,

Also a lesson we seemed to have learned the hard way: There is often more than ONE TRAIN STATION and chances are you're at the wrong one.

Yeah, remember Madrid in that savory country I could take or leave...

Oh yeah, it was their fault we were stupid 17 year olds

Euston, and caught the 21:45 train to Inverness. We got a whole compartment to ourselves so we could stretch out and sleep. It's a 14 hour train trip to save on accommodations.

Funny how when you're 17 comfort seems to be a valid trade-off with money.

I remember that whenever we got a compartment to ourselves we thought that was the best thing. Of course, as I look at some of our photos, it's no wonder we didn't draw a crowd!

I can just imagine.

No money or food. But I'm going to get some via wire at American Express.

Not totally true. I wasn't out of money...yet. According to the next day's entry I've still got $40 left...which in England should last till lunchtime the next day.

Man, according to my day's accounting (see today's entry from me), you were at $70 in Salisbury. Those brain teasers must have been expensive or maybe we had another Dunkin Donut moment. I do recall that your money situation was starting to get to you.

Yeah, you'll start to see me mention it more and more.

Although it doesn't get recorded, I think tomorrow, in Scotland is when we enjoyed that wonderful can of Van Kamp beans on the way to Loch Ness!

Uh oh. While I didn't record it either I remember the beans and I remember them specifically as Heinz beans. Blue and gray label. We opened them up with our handy-dandy Swiss army knives and ate them cold right out of the can on the way to the loch. I remember Dawn and Susi being thoroughly disgusted...and even more so that evening.

Now hold on a minute. Are you sure it was a can of Heinz beans? I remember using the Swiss Army knife (which I still have) to get the can open, but all I can see in my mind's eye is the reddish orange label...

No no no…quite certain they were Heinz. Remember it well. Blue/gray/green with the beans on the front. I remember being surprised that they had Heinz over there, and I was trying to remember if Heinz even made baked beans in the States.

POSTCARD: A nice little montage of Salisbury with five of the sights of the city (St. Annes' gate, the Market, Poultry Cross, High Street Gate, the Cathedral). Didn't send this one either but, once again, it's all addressed and ready to go. Notes on the back:

> #13 June 19, 1982
> Nice town - typically English

How arrogant...as if I'd been to all the English towns. Perhaps "Stereotypically English" would have been better.

And my thoughts were wandering to Thomas Hardy and Mr. Sanders English class...

- small but seems big

There I go again, the master of paradoxical vagueness.

- Saw everything on postcard.

Well big deal, we saw almost all of Paris in 36 hours, what else can you do?

On to Scotland!

Tony's Journal

June 20, 1982

We arrived in Inverness, Scotland at about 11:30. Walked around and found a campsite about a mile 1/2 away. We are staying here for Pound 1.50 per person ($3.00). We did nothing today but set up camp and take a nap. We got up and had some fish-n-chips for dinner and now we are just sitting around.

It is windy and cold at this camp, but it has a lot of things for general use.

Unlike those places we stayed earlier with all those SPECIALIZED items. "General use." WHAT THE HELL DOES THIS MEAN?

We are about 5 miles from Loch Ness and plan to walk down there tomorrow and maybe catch a glimpse of "Nessie".

Let's see, cost of the camp, nap, fish and chips, windy and cold....hmmm, well, um, due to the fact that: 1) this entry is very short and 2) it is remarkably like mine I find I have very few smart-ass comments to make that won't sound like the same smart ass comments I made about my own I guess I'm forced to let this one stand with just the one.

Butch's Journal

Day 20 - June 20, 1982 - Inverness, Scotland

We got here today at about 11:00. Called the campsite to make sure there was room.

As I recall, the place was huge and there were about 4 people there, none of them as stupid as us and living in tents but rather RVs. Does anyone else remember this?

Hey pal, I think it was 11:30, no wonder we got lost all the time, you must have been on Estonian time or something. I remember the place being good sized, but I don't recall a lot of Scottish RVs...

After getting a LITTLE lost

Geeeze. This happened so much to us I'm surprised I went through the trouble of recording it.

You know, I think the Harvard guys should have entitled their book, "Let's Get Lost" instead of "Let's Go Europe." Does anyone still have that book? I seem to recall it was in Mr. Bill's hands most of the time...

we made it here and bought a campsite. 3 pounds/tent. I only have $40 left. Gonna have to get some more. Windy and cold up here in the Scottish Highlands.

I don't know if we were in the Scottish Highlands, I think I just liked the way it sounded.

I thought all of Scotland was highlands. You know, Mel Gibson running around screaming at the English, whipping up the locals in his battle dress. Until he was drawn and quartered anyway...

After we finished setting up the tents we took a nap.

Despite all that great sleep we got on the train last night when we saved on accommodations.

I was thinking the same thing. Maybe it was the 'altitude', being in the highlands and so close to the North Pole and all. What was it? about 50 degrees at night?

Then we went to the fish 'n' chips place and had...fish 'n' chips.

Believe it or not I remember these fish 'n' chips. They had to be greasiest things I've ever eaten. They gave them to us in a paper cone-like construction and when I got to the bottom of the cone there was about an inch of grease, just sitting there. I think I recall hearing my left ventricle slamming shut.

It didn't leave me with the same impression. I guess I was just looking forward to a good can of cold beans...

We tried to get something in a bottle to warm our bones but couldn't find a place with take-away so we went cold and dry.

I find it hard to believe that we looked too hard as we were in the land of some of the most famous drinkers in the world.

Now this I remember vividly. I remember you and me conspiring to find a pub, offer them whatever you had left of your $40 for a whole

bottle of Scotch, no sissy single drinks for us Yanks. I mean, we figured every Scotsman must have been walking around with a bottle of booze. It's a good thing we didn't wander too far past the campground looking for a drink or there could have been trouble! We must have taken another nap instead.

Attempting to go to bed was fun. At 0:00 (when I fell asleep) it was still light, at 0:30 (that's when Tony went to sleep) it was still light, and when we woke up at three, lo and behold, it was light. It never gets dark here.

Sometimes my astuteness amazes me.

I have more on this in my entry tomorrow.

It really freaked me out.

Like...you know...wow.

Dawn on the celebrity-strewn beaches of Loch Ness

Tony's Journal

June 21, 1982

We seem to think that the sun may never set here in Scotland. It wasn't set at midnight or at 3 a.m. The four of us braved the cold and walked about 7 miles to the mouth of Loch Ness.

I am quite amazed that, despite how well the beans have stayed in our memory that neither of us mentions it here. We've spent the last few days discussing what brand of beans they were and it could have been easily settled had either of us chose to record this rather significant event.

We walked down a little ways but didn't see the monster. We walked back and all of us are aching somewhat. My left leg hurts some and I have a couple of blisters. We had a semi-warm dinner on the Ezbits tonite and have turned in rather early.

Awwwww, again with the cute little Ezbits. I remember that it was in Scotland on the way to the campsite that we passed a store that had Ezbit fuel in the window. You wanted to go back when it was open but we never did. This, along with the beans would have to the stupidest, least important thing I remember about the trip.

Butch called his mom and it looks as if he may get $100 when we get to Glasgow tomorrow.

Ahhh, part two of the Great $100 saga.

I think we definitely have to do some wash 'cause I'm down to my last pair of underwear.

Which should have lasted you another couple of weeks.

I liked my underwear...what can I say? I didn't get a rash from it or anything.

That's probably because it had become one with your body by the time you got around to changing them.

The walk, although a bit long, was refreshing enough. We saw some of the Scottish highlands and a lot of sheep. We walked between the Ness river and its canal.

I don't remember many sheep for some reason but I do remember the canal and the locks and the narrow boats along it. That walk really sticks in my memory.

We are all pooped for the most part which is good so we can get a good night's sleep before setting out early tomorrow.

I do remember that night too. I know I tossed and turned for seconds before nodding off.

One thing I noticed about the Scots I encountered was that they are all very friendly and very willing to help out.

Funny we both mentioned this, it *must* be so then if the bloody Colonists noticed it.

Well, we are praying for a dry night and wondering if the sun ever sets, especially on a cold first day of summer.

Butch's Journal

Day 21 - June 21, 1982 - Scotland, Inverness-Loch Ness

Today we walked (and walked and walked) 6 and a half miles to the loch. We looked for Nessie but she wasn't there today.

OK, enough of the sights, let's get on to the meaningless stuff.

I've got two pics from this part of the adventure. One with me, you and Susi with Loch Ness in the background (no Nessie) and the other of Dawn skipping stones on the rocky shore.

The Scotch

How very UN-PC of me: the SCOTS.

You had Scotch on the brain. You were trying to find a way to get a whole bottle of Scotch for 'general use.'

are very helpful and nice. On numerous occasions they've gone out of their way to help me. The old ladies at the phone,

Both sprang to their change purses when I asked if they had change for 20p as if in a race to give me the correct change.

I don't remember the old ladies in detail. But the Scots made an impression on me as well with their willingness to help.

the grass cutter,

Actually, I hated him. Just kidding. He gave us the directions to the Loch and then told us to say hello to "the beastie" for him.

the old couple downtown,

they let us mug them, it was great. Actually, I don't have any memory of some old couple so they couldn't have been that nice.

the young couple outside the campsite,

"Excuse us, do you know where the campground is?"
"The campground?"
"Yes."
"It's right behind ye."
"Oh, Thanks." (I think someone needs a nap).

all were instrumental in getting us to where we were going.

I think this is the melodramatic cliché edition of my journal entries.

There's a bird outside our tent that eats when we do and probably better than we do. He even eats out of my hand. It's cool.

Apparently there is a lot to do in and around Loch Ness.

I'd forgotten about the bird until you mentioned it. Let's see, a cat friend in Salisbury, a bird in Scotland...just as long as we didn't catch you with any sheep, I think we're OK. We could start a chapter called, "Let's Go Noah!"

It's really cold for Midsummer's Day,

See above melodramatic entry.

It* was *cold.

I mean COLD. (It's now 22:30 and I'm writing by the light of the midnight sun)

Again on the melodramatic thing...

I called my mom today to ask her to wire me some money through the Glasgow American Express from Munich. Only $100 cause that's all I should need. It's getting across on the damn ferries that costs so much.

A few years ago when Cracker put out their song "Eurotrash Girl" about an ill fated trip around Europe there was a line in there about calling his mom from a payphone because he was down to his last bit of money...It will always mean Scotland for me.

Ireland is next after a stop in Glasgow to, hopefully, pick up some money, it'll be on to Stranrear to catch a boat to Larne then to Belfast.

Marginal notes:

1) 14 stones to a pound, I weigh 11 stone.
2) 1 British Pint = 1.25 US Pints

I don't know what the hell is going on here. Someone must have given me some kind of conversion table to look at. LOTS to do in Loch Ness. AHHHH, to be 14 stone again...not a day goes by that I don't think of being 14 stone. Of course, when we started the trip I think I was 50 stone.

You know, even if that can of beans wasn't too filling, I think I would have noticed if you were down to about 14 pounds. Didn't you mean 14 pounds to a stone? I mean, I would have taken the

Let's Go book if I'd known it made up about 30% of weight by the time we hit Scotland! They say the hunger pains just go away after you've been starving. Maybe Dawn should have shared that Chicken with you in London...

Yes, you're quite right. Just trying to make myself seem thinner than I really was...it was 14 pounds to a stone.

Postcard: A nice one with a sunburst motif that says "Around Loch Ness". Castles, ruins, the loch and something I can't figure out. The back says:

> #14 June 21, 1982
> Cold and Windy-Never Gets Dark Here-At 3:00am it was light-we walked 13 miles to Loch Ness and back.

I'm starting to get the feeling that it was cold and windy and light in Scotland.

The sun never setting was a sight. But why were we up every three hours checking it out? Obviously because we were obsessed with it. Now you know why the ancient Celts and ancient people in general were in awe over the summer solstice. Oh how far civilization had come by 1982...there we were, in awe of old Sol. I'm surprised we didn't hustle back to Stonehenge for a Pagan dance with a head clearing mustard chaser!!

Tony's Journal

June 22, 1982

> *We got up around 7 and caught the train to Glasgow. When we got here we found out that it takes three days for a wire money order. So, Mrs. Cook is sending a postal money order which takes two days and will meet Butch in Dublin.*

The plot thickens.

> *Now we are sitting in a small coffee shop. Lady Diana's child was born and it was a boy.*

Big follower of the Royals, huh? I remember this too. It was front page on seemingly everything. Wonder why I didn't note it.

Me and the Royals go way back. Lots of memorable things happened when I was involved with them.

> *Today on the train Butch and I played at least 50 hands of UNO. The girls played with their LOGIC books. It helped pass the four hour train ride pretty much though. We are taking the 2200 train to Belfast tonight, so we had about 8 hrs to kill. But since there wasn't much to see here in Glasgow, we stayed close to the station.*

You know, I'll bet there is plenty to do in Glasgow, but after the big Loch Walk the day before I'm sure it was very easy to convince

ourselves that there wasn't.

We are kinda getting pressed for time and may have to skip the Scandinavian countries.

Were they really on the agenda at all? That would probably be on that map we made before we left, not on the one I have. I don't recall ever thinking we could make that but I've always wanted to go up there. It's the only area of Western Europe I never made it to.

The ferry ride is gonna cost us, but we don't know how much for sure yet. Everybody is in good spirits I guess.

Considering everyone is tired, broke, and odorous.

Butch & I had a beer and the girls have been drinking tea. Hopefully, we'll be in Ireland tomorrow morning.

And wasn't that arrival a treat.

Butch's Journal

Day 22 - June 22, 1982 - Inverness - Glasgow Scotland

We got up at about 06:00 this morn. Susi and Dawn took a shower but Tony and I didn't.

I'll bet I can guess something else Tony didn't do…it involves underwear. We seem like good, hygienic little boys. We walked 13 miles yesterday, slept in a sleeping bag, we've got 2 full days of traveling ahead of us in close quarters on a train....nahhhh, we don't need a shower.

We broke camp and made the long trek to the train station. We saw the castle that Macbeth murdered King Duncan in. The original is gone but this one is on the same place.

This is twice I've discussed a fictional event as if it were real. Must be all the comic books I had read and my heightened suspension of disbelief.

The mayor of Inverness once refused entrance to Mary Queen of Scots. Even though he changed his mind the next day, he was executed.

Why would I include this?

Executions do tend to stand out.

We ate bacon burgers and chips and tea.

The breakfast of champions.

That's my Sunday morning meal...it's not everyone's?

The train to Glasgow left at 10:20 and we got to Glasgow at 14:05, we walked to the right station and one the way stopped at the American Express to see about my money. They said a cable takes 3 days so I called my mom (on a broken booth and it cost me only 20p for about 15 min) and she said she'll send an American Express money order to Dublin American Express.

I remember this first stop on the Great Money Trek. I was really starting to get worried.

I remember there being snags for this $100. It probably cost your mom as much to wire it out. Now if it were today, we'd just whip over to an ATM and be done with it. No need to carry cash anywhere, just walk over the ATM and there you have it. Of course, Dawn's sitting on about $200, but there's no way you'll see any of it, buster. You'll rot in an Irish pauper's prison before we'd help you. Dawn, did we ever talk about bailing Butch out, or were we having too much fun watching him sweat? Why didn't we just throw one of our awesome hats down in the train station and sing for a few quid?

Actually, Dawn did lend me $20 which I note a little later in my journal when I paid her back (at least, that's how I'll write it here). When I talked to Dawn last week she was quite surprised that she had as much money as she did and didn't give me any, she was equally surprised when I told her she did as she had no memory of either giving it to me or having it to give. It did refresh her memory a bit when she remembered that I had to carry her pack and go get her food for those last few days.

We have to wait until 22:00 for our train. No big deal. We have to catch another ferry over to Ireland which should cost about 3.75pounds.

I remember this night very well due to the "fast food" steak and kidney pie I had at the ferry just before boarding. It was "fast food" because you could hold it in your hand and eat it!! As if I should have wanted to. At that point, however, I think haggis would have looked good.

We should get into Belfast about 07:00.

Tony's Journal

June 23, 1982

Our ferry was a little bit late but nothing major. We got to Belfast and everyone started talking it down & how sorry it looked and how they couldn't wait to leave. So, we left right away from there to go to Dublin.

Yeah, big talker. Nice to see you're more honest now than then.

I didn't want to hurt your feelings. I was just one of the four, after all!

It was interesting because we had to get out of our train and change to a bus because somebody threatened to blow up that particular run. Once we got into the Irish Republic we got back onto a train.

La la la la. No big deal. A total of four lines in two journals.

We came to Dublin and checked our stuff in so we could walk around a little bit. We ate well at the Burger King.

An oxymoron if I ever saw one.

Afterwards Butch

A moron if I ever saw one.

decided to get his hair cut and he did. It looks good, I think. He thinks it could be longer in back, but I feel it could even be shorter and still look good.

So, does someone pay everyone in my life to say things like that? I did find some pics taken soon after our return and, you're right, it isn't really very short, unless you compare it to what I had. But it was my security blanket and help sustain that Jesus complex I had.

After that we got accommodations at a hostel w/ a dorm. Irish Pound 2.50 ($3.50). The beds aren't the greatest but it's a place to sleep.

It's funny we both have a line like this. Our standards got lower and lower as the trip progressed. I guess anything beats a bench in an Italian train station. (I know I've probably referenced that before but it was a pivotal event in my young life).

The girls aren't too excited about the place.

I'm shocked....SHOCKED.... to find this out!

Once we were settled we decided to look for some sights in Dublin. We saw some churches, the big Post Office and Trinity College. We saw a play, "Sleuth", which was pretty good. It's pretty cool in the Republic because everything is in Gaelic first, then English. The weather is still miserable.

You know though, I remember this being a very relaxing stop. It just seemed so peaceful there (especially compared to someone threatening to blow us up) and I really enjoyed it.

I'm getting a royal cold, too. Tomorrow we hope to get to Cork for the night. Depends on how things go. Not really all that much to see in Dublin, but it's nice to be in the land of my ancestors.

Isn't this what you said about France? Pick an ethnicity and run with it there Savageau.

Well, I did have a mom and a dad…and their parents were not related, to my knowledge.

So you say.

All is very green here like they say.

Including the beds at the hostel if I remember correctly.

Still having fun although this cold came at a bad time. Looking forward to the rest. I'm very tired right now and turning in at 11:00 p.m. That's about it for now I guess. So long till tomorrow.

And you were talking to WHO here? Us 15 years later?

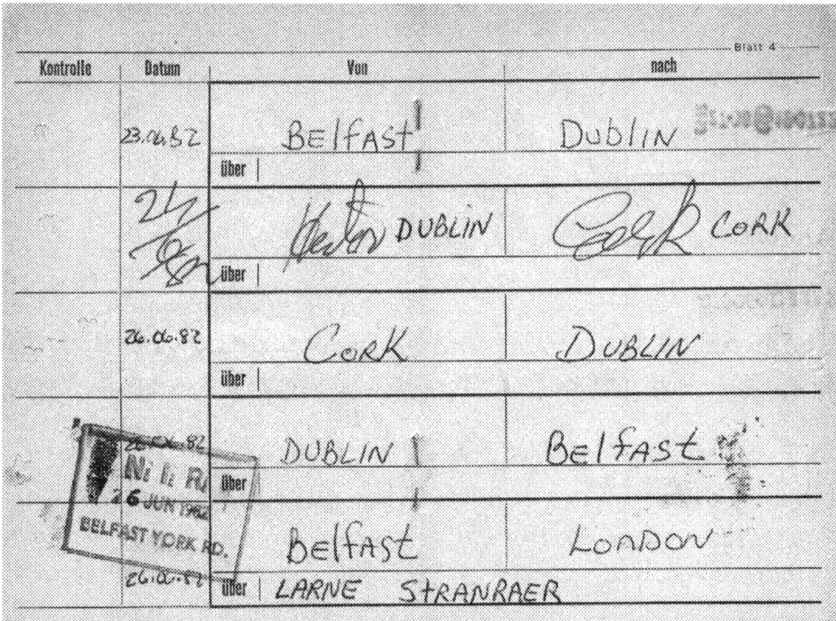

Blatt 4

Kontrolle	Datum	Von	nach
	23.06.82	Belfast	Dublin
	über		
	24/6	DUBLIN	CORK
	über		
	26.06.82	Cork	Dublin
	über		
NIR 26 JUN 1982 BELFAST YORK RD.	26.06.82	DUBLIN	Belfast
	über		
		Belfast	London
	26.06.82 über	LARNE STRANRAER	

Butch's Journal

Day 23 - June 23 - 1982 Belfast to Dublin, Ireland

The ferry was late so we got into Belfast late. It was spooky, rainy, cold and no one wanted to stay. I didn't care and neither did Tony so we went to Dublin instead.

Boy, do I remember this well. A gray morning, we walked out of the station and around the corner and saw the wall around the city and the military vehicles and the checkpoints and turned around and left. On a sunny morning perhaps the trappings of imperialism and military occupation might have seemed a little more festive but I think it caught us a little off guard.

I actually remember being a little miffed that you guys didn't want to wander around a little longer. But, it was bleak, gray and felt like a prison.

In Dublin the first thing we did was check our baggage and look for the tourist office. From there we went to Burger King when I decided to get my hair cut at the place next door.

I remember I just couldn't stand the shit hanging in my eyes all the time...of course, it probably would have helped if I had taken the opportunities offered me during the trip to wash it every now and again.

We should all buy stock in Burger King. It seems to have been our eating place of choice no matter where we found ourselves. I'd

forgotten about your hair cut until I got to this point. I've got a few pictures of you 'before' and 'after'. It looks good, and I wouldn't exactly call is short. Now, were you just getting giddy thinking about all the dough your mom was going to send you and you decided to splurge on a hair cut!

Yeah, but with all that hair I'm surprised he didn't want to give me an estimate first and then come back.

The cutter, Ross, was a little on the HAPPY side but he cut my hair ok.

See, that's my oh-so clever, 17 year old, early 80's way of saying he was gay. And then I make a point of saying that, despite this fact, he cut my hair ok, because, you know, who ever heard of a gay hair stylist? How young and foolish I was.

Then, after picking up our baggage, we went to the International Student Assn/Activity Centre (I.S.A.A.C.). No one liked it. Granted it's not the best, a little seedy and expensive (2.50 pounds) but it suffices as a place to lay your head.

I think my need for a bed, a real live bed (which is what they turned out to be if I remember Tony's story correctly) blinded me momentarily. Upon retrospect the place looked a bit like that prison in *Midnight Express*.

My story involves a hallmate of mine from college. Turns out he was camping through Ireland the same time we were and stayed at the same dump we did, within days of when we were there. We only came away with bad memories, he left with pubic lice! Then again, maybe it was more like a Turkish prison than we suspected, especially since the guys and gals were separated...

From there we tried to go to the city center. Never made it I don't think. We went to the main Post Office and bought some stamps and tried to find St. Patrick's Church. No such luck. We made a big circle

Couldn't find anything, walking around in circles....it might be time for us to think about heading home.

and came out at Grafton Street right across from Trinity College. We went inside and saw an ad for a play being put on - Sleuth - not with Sir Laurence Oliver and Michael Caine but very, very good.

I purchased this movie not long ago because we saw this play. I remember the night we first saw the film at Tony's and being really impressed...the play was less impressive but we felt so cultural seeing a play in Ireland.

The train from Belfast to Dublin was threatened by a bomb threat

"...threatened by a bomb threat"...? I find that redundantly redundant.

so we unloaded before the border and took a bus across and got back on the train. Scary.

I like how I stuck this in as an afterthought. Like, "oh yeah, someone said they were gonna blow me up." I do remember not being so much scared as excited. I just thought this was really cool, us, caught up in the political intricacies of a decades old skirmish. Kinda glad nothing happened though now that I think about it in retrospect. Would have probably ruined what was left of the trip.

Tomorrow, after I pick up my money, and go see the Guinness Brewery and have a pint or two, we're going to Cork City where, hopefully, there's a hostel with BATHS

Oh, NOW I'm all interested in taking a bath. Where was this interest when we were at a place with running water?

Once you visited the gang showers above, anyone would welcome a bath!

Actually, I don't remember the gang showers. Did I take one? That doesn't sound like me at that age. As Woody Allen said in "Annie Hall" when asked why he didn't take a shower at the tennis club: "I never take group showers. I don't like to be naked in front of other men of my gender."

plus the Blarney Stone in Blarney Castle. May skip that though.

Since I remember going to Blarney Castle I wonder if that means I skipped the bath?

Marginal notes: Only two. the exchange rate: "Irish pounds to dollars: 1.49 pounds = $1.00" **and a note that this was everyone's 17 month anniversary.**

Awwwwwwwww...

(Editor's Note: Tony and Dawn's anniversary was January 23, 1981...as was Butch and Susi's, though not by design. Thereafter, for the length of the respective relationships, 23rds were held in high regard. Hardly seems like the kind of thing to mention in a book of this nature, but it is done so as to explain the above marginal note.)

Tony's Journal

June 24, 1982

We left our bed today and set out for Heuston station on the other side of town. We checked our luggage at the station and set out for the world famous Guinness Brewery. We went through the museum and sampled some of their double stout for free.

Free Stout...it's a wonder you guys ever got me out of there. The local brew-pub has an Oatmeal Stout that reminds me a lot of the Guinness we had that day. None of the countless Guinnesses (Guinnessi?) I've had since ever tasted as good as that stuff we had at the brewery.

You say "double-stout" – I don't make mention of that...was it really some special double-stout?

Also inside we got to see a one man, for the most part, skit on the life, I guess of James Joyce. It was very interesting and well done. We saw a brief movie about how the brew is made too. From there we walked over to St. Patrick's Cathedral where Jonathan Swift is buried and walked around a bit.

I'm glad you record this because I didn't. All these years I could have been bragging to all the rubes in the VCU English Dept. about being at the church where Jonathan Swift is buried and I missed it.

Wait...who's Jonathan Swift...?

Leaving there, we went to the American Express to see about Butch's money.

Yes, yes, yes. Butch's Money, Butch's Rash, Butch's Money, Butch's Rash...

It hadn't come. So, we went back to Hueston and wrote some post cards and caught the 17:30 train to Cork. Butch and I played UNO almost the whole way. We got to Cork and I found two Brynes listed in the phone books.

A little explanation here would be nice.

The Brynes were my Irish relatives on my mother's side of the family. It's a unique spelling of the Irish last name, and I've almost never seen it spelled that way, except while we were in Ireland. But, my Brynes were Orange Irish, despite being from the area around Cork.

We are staying in a B&B across from the train station for about Irish Pound 6.00 ($8.50) per person. But that's w/ a shower and breakfast. We met a girl from California named Bonnie at the train station who came along and is sharing a room w/ Dawn & Susi. She seems nice enough and we all talked for about an hour.

But WHAT did we talk about? Someone has to have recorded more about this person!

Butch and I are sharing a room as are the girls.

I'm sure our mothers will be quite happy to hear that.

We hope to do some wash tomorrow as there is a launderette nearby.

"Launderette"? I see the UK speech pattern is rubbing off on you. A little James Joyce in a brewery and suddenly you're....ummm....Jonathan Swift.

My cold isn't any better and it bugs me. This is a real nice and homey place we are staying in.

I wonder if it really was or was it just nice relative to everywhere else we had stayed? I mean, if you go to just about any town in the world the places to stay that are right across the street from the train station are seldom the nicest places in town. I mean, remember that pension we stayed in in Milan when the cops chased us out of the waiting room at the station? It was nice enough compared to the numerous benches and sleeping bags we had slept in and on for the previous couple of days, but, really, it wasn't all that great. However, that being said, I do also remember the B&B in Ireland being very cozy and comfortable.

Nice old lady who runs the place is very helpful. Gonna be nice to sleep in a nice bed and have a real breakfast. Tomorrow we hope to go to Blarney Castle and

'Scuze me, while I...

kiss the stone.

Butch's Journal

Day 24 - June 24, 1982 - Dublin to Cork, Republic of Ireland

We left I.S.A.A.C.

But did it leave us?

Yeah, hindsight tells us we were lucky...

this morning and hiked to the train station all the way across town. We checked our luggage and went around the block to the Guinness Brewery. We looked at the James Joyce exhibition and went the bar and had a half pint (not bad stuff that)

Food of the Gods.

Now, I've got a photo of you sitting in between Susi and Dawn all tipping the glass o'brew. I haven't had a Guinness since. Maybe I'm saving myself for Dublin return trip.

then we saw an hour long show about James Joyce. It was really interesting. One man did different parts of Joyce's books.

Of which I had read none at that point.

I don't remember the Joyce thing. I still haven't read any Joyce.

After that we saw a movie on the brewing of Guinness and I bought a tankard.

Which I still had until about 2 years ago when it was appropriated by person or persons unknown.

After that we hoofed it to the American Express where my money wasn't.

Seems like I recall us thinking that it really couldn't be there yet but we were hoping that, somehow, the money made it there in under 2 days. Hope springs eternal when you're broke.

Then we hoofed it back to the station and caught our train. In Cork we met this girl from California named Bonnie.

But HOW did we meet her? Why was she traveling alone? Why did she tag along with us? I wish I had recorded that. I hope that either you Tony or you Dawn did.

Nope. I didn't even recall the girls bunking in with her.

She looks really familiar.

Which, after many years of hearing myself say that, I have realized is my own secret code to myself that I probably find that person attractive. However, for the life of me I can't remember what this girl looked like.

She's traveling Eurail and went the almost opposite route we did. She tagged along. She and the girls are sharing a room and Tony and I are sharing. It's a b&b for 5.50 pounds and 50p for shower.

Why that's nearly TEN BUCKS!!! No wonder I was broke throwing

money around like that. I do remember it was a pretty comfortable place however.

Talk about going from darkness into the light. We went from the worst place we stayed on our trip to the best (and most expensive). It wasn't a bad deal though, considering you got a full, hot, Irish breakfast. However, you must have been down to your last few pence.

Not really bad.

Yeah, see if you're saying that when you're selling your plasma for food money to make it home there Richie Rich.

We all (Bonnie included) have to wash clothes tomorrow then we all may go see Blarney Castle and kiss the Blarney Stone for that gift of gab. We're leaving Saturday morning EARLY (about 05:00) so we can get to the American Express.

Uh-oh. My money problems starting to change the schedule. However, I may point out something here that hasn't be recorded, at least in my journal: there was a pending rail strike in the UK fast approaching and everyone knew it. After Spain, had we stayed ONE DAY longer anywhere we would have been stuck in the UK, with the country sucking every last pence out of us. So, my money problems forcing us to Dublin a little early was actually a really good thing and you don't have to thank me for it.

Listen to Mr. Spinmaster. I think we did spend one day too long in Spain and as I look at the pics we spent a heck of a long time in the U.K. We could have made it to Scandinavia if we'd cut out Ireland. I'm glad we didn't though. Notice that our Irish entries seem to be the longest and detailed. I think I get to the strike at some point. I do remember it causing us some angst.

Then we're going straight to Amsterdam if all goes right.

Which it must have because I do remember us being in Amsterdam.

Yeah, by way of Brugge...

Susi, Butch, Dawn - sitting down for a little break at the Guiness brewery - sadly, the picture of Butch being dragged away kicking and screaming was lost.

Tony's Journal

June 25, 1982

First off this morning we had a very filling breakfast that consisted of cereal, eggs, bacon, sausage, toast, bread, butter, jam, juice and tea. Delicious.

We were living large at a point when we had the least money. Actually, it's at this point when my memory becomes the most fuzzy. The last few days of the trip are very confusing, probably because we were in a mad dash to beat the strike out of the UK, or perhaps, overcome by all the luxury we became fat and lazy.

DAWN: It's at this point that I remember the most (probably some sort of second wind)

Probably clearing up as you were excited that the trip was almost over.

Then the four of us went in our shorts and did the wash. Felt good to put on some clean underwear.

Which means that it must have been a full moon that night since your underwear changing schedule seemed to be on a lunar cycle.

DAWN: As I recall, you had no skivvies on under those shorts when we went to do wash, figuring 'Hey - If I'm gonna wash em, I'm gonna wash em all.'

Right, much the same philosophy was behind the reason I went to the Laundromat naked.

I was practicing my frugal Yankee persona. I was going to need it…and my underwear.

> *After that we walked about the shops in town and ate at Pizzaland. In my hurry, mostly, to catch a bus to Blarney, Dawn and I got into a little spat.*

I neither recorded this nor do I remember it. It must have happened when we went to get the tickets and you went to the store together.

DAWN: Mr. Sniffles was getting on my nerves, I guess.

Mr. Sniffles? I was an iron man! Except for my cold, shin splints, hunger pangs, and short temper…OK…maybe I complained a few times…but at least I didn't get a splinter on the second day!

> *We got the 1600 bus to Blarney where we went into the woolen shop and spent about an hour. Dawn got a sweater, me a T-shirt, Butch a sweat shirt and Susi nothing.*

Any idea what was on the sweat shirt? I don't remember it.

DAWN: I believe it said "Went to Ireland and all I could afford was this lousy t-shirt."

And your sweater said, if I recall correctly, "Why yes, I DO have all the money."

> *Walking to the castle we discovered Dawn had lost her camera. Tempers flew again and she was really upset. So was I because it was 3 weeks of pictures.*

That's funny, I don't remember that part either. I remember Dawn being disappointed that she lost the camera, but I don't recall any tempers flying or anything like that. However, keep in mind my previous comments about my memories at this time getting a little fuzzy.

DAWN: Disappointed? I was devastated! Didn't you guys know you should never let me carry important stuff....like a camera? That's why I never got to hold "THE BOOK."

Those photos were so important…it took you five months to get them developed! But I'm glad you did, it's the only photographic record we have.

First, I think I let you touch the book...once. Second, I was protecting everyone by carrying the book. There are tests you have to take and other books you have to read, and the "Let's Go" people have employees stationed throughout Europe that will walk up to the person carrying a current copy of "Let's Go" and begin quizzing them and if you don't get all the answers right, they take it away from you. Right then and there. It doesn't matter that it was Tony's book, it's whoever is holding it. I spent months preparing for that. You don't have to thank me for the hell it put me through...

...actually, I think I just really liked leading everyone around.

That's certainly what we wanted you to think. Carrying the extra five pounds that book represented was good enough for me.

Anyway, after a futile search we walked up to the castle and walked around inside. We went up and kissed the Blarney stone and all acquired the gift of gab. It was cool. We walked down to catch the bus and there was one waiting there. Because Susi wanted to explore some woods or something

See, see! It's all Susi's fault. All of it. Of course, should Susi ever get involved with this reconstruction we'll put it to a vote and see what she remembers but right now I'm going with the "it's Susi's fault" story.

DAWN: O.K. I like the "Susi's fault" story. I'm going with that too (although we all know whose fault it REALLY was - see my comments to Mr. Bill's Journal 6/25).

Susi, did you get the number of the bus Dawn and Mr. Bill were driving? Did you?

> *She and Butch weren't there so we missed that one and the next one was too late for us to catch the musical we had tickets for. However, some good came out of it because I asked the driver what time the next bus left and discovered it was the same bus we got there in. They had Dawn's camera. Relief and the tensions were eased.*

Wait a minute. Maybe I should claim some of the credit...uh...blame for us missing the bus. Because "I" made us miss the bus you guys found the camera and there is a photographic record of this trip. See, I was hoping that if we walked around in the woods a little bit it would give you guys the chance to search some more for Dawn's camera. Obviously I was correct and please don't feel that you have to thank me for it 15 years later. (Good to know that Blarney Stone is still working).

DAWN: Well, you've gone 15 years without a photographic record, Mr. Bill. I don't believe that explanation holds any water.

No, but see, I always knew the photos were there, that was enough for me.

But we still had 55 minutes to get 5 miles in order to see our Irish Pound 3.50 musical. So, we decided to hitch. We walked a little way before a VW bus w/ some freaky looking Germans picked Dawn and I up and a bit later Susi & Mr. Bill, who had opted to walk ahead. They were OK and got us to Cork w/ 25 minutes to spare.

Buddha Provides.

DAWN: Actually, the freaky looking Germans were thinking they could steal the camera from the "freaky looking Americans."

Hey, who are you calling "freaky"? My hair was freshly coifed (and I think we all know how painful that can be).

And I'm pretty sure my shorts were buried deep in my backpack by now, since it never seemed to get out of the 40's while we were in the British Isles.

The musical was called The Pirates of Penzance and was quite good. I enjoyed it.

You know, I remember it vividly and it really was really good wasn't it? I remember it being a really big production and being impressed at its size and the colors and the guys swinging from ropes in the rafters. It definitely seems to have lifted the spirits of the writer of this journal entry.

DAWN: So what good was the camera anyway? I didn't take any pictures of this theatrical blockbuster.

I'm sure there was a no camera policy. Besides, we probably gave the camera to Mr. Bill so you wouldn't lose it again.

From there we walked to a Kentucky Fried Chicken to take home

"Home" seems to be anywhere with indoor plumbing in your journal.

I can think of two KFC's in all of Eastern Mass...how come there was one wherever we turned in Europe? I guess they love their fried chicken. I remember seeing a KFC when I stepped off the plane at my honeymoon spot and thinking how in the world can there be a KFC in Aruba!

a little dinner. It was 10:30 p.m. We got home and talked in the girls room where Bonnie was waiting up for a little while.

I'm sure it was me she was waiting up for. (Hey, it's 15 years later and we don't even know her last name, I can say anything about her I want).

DAWN: I believe it was Susi she was waiting up for (not that there's anything WRONG with that).

You know, in the long run I would have to say that the only thing this trip lacked was even more attractive lesbians hitting on my girlfriend. But, god knows, when do you ever get enough of that?

We have to wake up early (0400) and catch the 0510 train to Dublin. Fun, fun, fun!!! Good night, I'm tired.

DAWN: Do you remember that "fun, fun, fun" expression from high school? Did we all say it?

No, I think we all made fun of the folks that did....I mean, except you Dawn.

CORK OPERA HOUSE

Secretary — Thomas Donnelly Tel. 20022/23680

COMMENCING MONDAY, 14th JUNE, 1982

Nightly at 8.00 **Saturday Matinees at 2.30**

NOEL PEARSON presents

THE NEW PRODUCTION OF GILBERT & SULLIVAN'S

" THE PIRATES OF PENZANCE "

THE CAST (in order of appearance)

PIRATE KING ....

SAMUEL, his lieutenant ....

FREDERIC ....

RUTH, a Pirate Maid ....

MAJOR-GENERAL STANLE

EDITH ....

KATE ....

ISABEL ....

MABEL ....

MAJOR-GENERAL STANLE

OPERA HOUSE

FRIDAY, June 25

STALLS

NIGHT

S 9

Ticket available only for date and time stated

HB To be retained

Butch's Journal

Day 25 - June 25, 1982 - Cork City, Ireland

After my shower this morn

Yaayyyyy! A recorded act of personal hygiene!!!

It was probably because I was obsessed with clean underwear! I must have finally worn you down.

DAWN: Hey, what's the deal with the clean underwear? I offered you a clean pair of mine several times throughout the trip. Mr. Bill found them to be acceptable,

And still do.

DAWN: and they fit him perfectly fine. Was it the colors you didn't like? (A little known fact...not only did I have the most money...I also had the most underwear!)

I'm not sure it was the underwear in your backpack I was hoping you'd offer up...but I do want to hear more about Mr. Bill's acceptability of them!!

I went down and had the best breakfast we've had all trip.

Better than bacon burgers in Scotland? ....hard to believe.

No, you can see in my journal that I was quite impressed with breakfast as well. I recorded every item on the table. It was quite a spread. That's me, always thinking about our next meal and my clean underwear.

DAWN: Yes! THE BREAKFAST! Although I don't remember much, I do remember that wonderful breakfast!

> Bonnie ate with us then we split up, and the 4 of us went to wash our clothes. After that, and an unsuccessful attempt to find the tourist office, we went back to Clon-Ross B&B to sort it all out.

I have a pretty strong memory of this event: when we went back to the B&B to sort out the clothes we dumped them all on one of the beds. Apparently, to save money, we all put our clothes together. Anyway, we were sorting out the whites (which, if i recall, no one's really were anymore) and Dawn held up a pair of my tidy whities which were stained red from The Red Sweatshirt Incident and green from my nappy rash medicine and proclaimed them as Mr. Bill's Christmas Underwear. I wore them for the yuletide season for years after. I suppose that should be embarrassing if I got embarrassed about things like that.

Now I, Mr. Underwear, have no recollection of this event! You do mention Bonnie quite a bit though. I don't even remember what she looked like.

DAWN: I don't believe Bonnie would have been interested in you Mr. Bill. I will have to consult my journal for any comments I may have made regarding this. Couldn't get my journal out of storage by myself without being crushed to death by falling boxes piled ten high! Going back with a squad of friends tomorrow. I remember that nappy rash medicine being on EVERYTHING! Why on earth would we wash our stuff with yours? Must have been a money issue.

Then we went to the bus depot to see how much it cost to go to Blarney Castle. From there we went to Pizzaland for some crappy pizza.

I don't know what gave us the idea that a place called Pizzaland would have adequate pizza. There must not have been a Burger King in town.

No, but we get to our second most popular joint for dinner, later.

Then we went into ALL the shops on the main drag looking for I don't know what, stuff I guess. Then, after going to the tourist office, we kinda split up. Susi and I went to the opera house to see about getting tickets to *The Pirates of Penzance*

Ahhhhh, and now the plot thickens....this is where I remember Tony getting a bit miffed....I can't wait to read the journal entry for this day.

I think you're a little pre-mature with miffedness. I don't recall getting PO'd yet, but I did record that Dawn and I got into a 'spat'. About what, I have no idea...Dawn?

DAWN: I believe it had something to do with your being such a damn baby about your sniffles. I'm sure I did my best to show you much warmth and compassion in your hours of need.

Yeah, my Iron Man-ness aside…I'm not sure warmth and compassion was in anyone's cards during our trip. Uno anyone?

and Tony and Dawn went back to some store. Susi and I bought 4 tickets (2 upstairs, 2 downstairs) for 3.50 pounds, a little expensive I guess.

See, I knew they were expensive, but I thought it would be a lot of fun....and, as I recall, it was.

That was expensive considering we were all down to mere pennies. I think this extravagant spending, combined with the next episode or two added to the boiling cauldron. Don't forget, I was suffering greatly from the sniffles...

Hey, that we managed to make it 25 days without a blow up of any kind (that got recorded anyway - and we haven't seen the rest of our journals yet) I'd say was pretty good. Plus, it seems to be rather minor one that the quality of the play seems to have overtaken.

DAWN: Enough about your sniffles, o.k., Tony? Who sat upstairs and who downstairs?

I think we sat upstairs. I remember looking down from the balcony.

> The play was at 22:00 so before that we went to Blarney Castle. We went into the woolen shop where Dawn bought a sweater for 33.00 pounds and I bought a Guinness sweatshirt for 5.00 pounds.

Theater tickets, sweatshirts....I knew I had that c-note just lying around there in Dublin and just became Imelda Marcos at Kinney's (how's that for a nice mid-80's reference?) Let's see if we can guess who still had the most money....ummm....I bought a $7.50 sweatshirt, Tony a cheap t-shirt and no record Susi buying anything, and Dawn bought a $50 sweater. And she STILL had the most money even after buying it!

I remember walking around this place for quite a while. An hour I think I recorded. I don't think I have my T-shirt. Dawn's wearing her new sweater in the last picture I have of the trip.

DAWN: Hey, I went on that trip specifically to get an Irish wool sweater, o.k? Those Irish sheep make one nice sweater! If any of you had wanted one, I would have been happy to buy it for you. I remember the store very well. The sweater I bought was on a shelf just to the left of the door. I also remember you guys getting pretty mad because I was taking so long. I brought it to college, pulled it down from the shelf in my dorm room and found that the moths also loved Irish wool.

> Then we explored the castle and Dawn discovered she lost her camera. Anyway, we explored the castle and kissed the Blarney stone. Me first, then Susi, Tony, and Dawn. We missed the bus we needed to take, but Tony and Dawn talked to the driver and Dawn got her camera back.

Bittersweet huh? I can't WAIT to read Dawn's entry for this day.

OK, here's the trouble brewing in Paradise (remember that concert? anyway...). OK, we have the 'spat' I referenced earlier in the day. We've spent big bucks on tickets and textiles.

But really, the tickets were only $5.00....not that I feel I have to rationalize anything after 15 years but, you know, a sawbuck one way or another probably wasn't going to kill us.

Dawn lost the camera and I'm sure I did my best to make her feel worse than she did. You nonchalantly mention that we missed the bus, but I recorded that it was clearly because Susi and you were lollygagging in the woods for God knows what.

As stated before, since Susi is the only one not currently participating in this reconstruction I'm more than willing to put forth the motion that she is totally to blame for us missing the bus. All in favor?

We missed the first bus and were gonna blow our money on the show, because we weren't going to make it there on time! But, with a bit of Irish luck on our side, the fates were there, that delay allowed us to recover our memories. And if I remember correctly, Dawn practically smothered the conductor with affection for finding the camera (much more affection than was going on in our tent at the time, if I remember...Dawn?)

DAWN: You know, as I read your entry about the camera, I thought to myself 'some things never change.' To this day (ask any of my friends) I seem to be a bit absentminded when it comes to holding onto things. So whatever you guys did to me on that trip to make me that way, I just want you to know that it's something I will live with for the rest of my life!!!!! Tony, you were so blindly sweet to record that we missed the bus "clearly because Susi and Mr. Bill were lollygagging in the woods for God knows what." Mr. Bill you were equally as sweet for not saying "Well, if Dawn hadn't spent an hour buying that Irish wool sweater, we wouldn't have missed the bus" (which is what we were all thinking.) As for the affection comment....I didn't think you could handle any affection, what with your 'sniffles' and all.

Always looking out for my well being...I appreciate it. But, I would have let you play nurse to my plague racked body if only you'd brought your tuffy tooth model from your dental assistant days.

There was a Mackey's Grill in Cork near Blarney.

I guess a note here would be good: My mother's maiden name was Mackey and I had always been told that the name was Scots-Irish and a corruption of the name MacKey so I was quite surprised to find the name, uncorrupted yet correct, just sitting there on a greasy spoon in County Cork.

We hitched back from Blarney and we got picked up by a VW van driven by a bunch of Belgian-Germans.

I can't believe I give this such little attention. I remember we split up because we thought it would be a lot easier for 2 people to get picked up rather than 4. Susi and I set off first and you guys were about 5 minutes behind us. When Susi and I saw the microbus slowing down we thought you guys had already been picked up by a previous car. Imagine our surprise when the side door slid open and you guys were right there. I remember the inside of the van looked like a set from a Cheech and Chong movie. I remember thinking that I cut my hair just a couple of days too soon. I remember them being quite nice however.

Yeah, Dawn and I were being SO gracious as to let you go ahead of us. Knowing full well that any car would go by us first and possibly pick us up before you. We told the freaks to drive on by you, but they didn't. Only kidding, we actually told them we were friends and would they be so kind as to pick you up too, we'd all make our play on time.

DAWN: Yeah, we thought no one would pick us up if they saw you first, Mr. Bill, you long-haired hippie freak! Was that van psychedelic on the outside? I really have a sixties-type flashback about this van and the people inside. Were they smoking marijuana? Maybe it was my imagination. I don't recall being too crazy about the fact that we had to hitchhike. I may have had my eyes closed inside the van the whole time.

I thought it was pretty rude of you to refuse their offer of periwinkles and squid for a snack, too.

We got to the theater just in time. After the show, which was quite good,

And I would know because, you know, I simply live for the theater.

DAWN: It was no match for the James Joyce reading though.

We were becoming quite the critics. It must have been that Shakespeare influence back in London and all.

DAWN: I suspect you mean theater critics and not food critics

we went to KFC for some chicken.

Oh good, we almost went a whole 2 days without some American fast food.

KFC, number two on the list of must eats in Europe. Right after the BK lounge of course.

And let us not forget that great health food restaurant we often frequented in the mornings: Dunkin' Donuts.

We took it back to the hostel and ate with Bonnie. I gave Bonnie my *Let's Go* book to use in London.

Don't worry Tony, it wasn't the Orange Bible, it was the 1980 edition of Let's Go Britain and Ireland that I had found in the tourist office in Belfast two summers before when I was there with my family.

So you were lugging around about 15 pounds of travel books? Nice.

However, now that I remember it was a 1980 edition I gave Bonnie, things are becoming a little clearer as to why we couldn't find anything.

Bonnie, Bonnie, Bonnie. You've mentioned her more than Susi the last few days pal.

Yeah, well, there wasn't much going on in our tent either.

You're just trying to make me feel better. Dawn, how was Bonnie as a roommate? Why was she waiting up for everyone, huh?

DAWN: She was a great roommate. Of course, we could have had Jack the Ripper for a roommate that night - it wouldn't have mattered we were so tired.

She said she'd send it back.

Which she never did.

She brought it back to CA as a souvenir of the night she stayed with the Euro based American travelers.

Doesn't matter, that's one less book I have to carry around.

Right, because I was so busy carrying YOURS around, Tony, and doing my best Al Haig impression: "I'M in charge!" (Wow, the second Big 80's reference).

I'm gonna look around for that book. Once you mentioned that I kept it, it seems I remember seeing somewhere, I'm not sure where. Al Haig gets a mention in my journal too.

Tomorrow we leave at 05:10 for Dublin to pick up my money and eventually get to Amsterdam.

Eventually is right. We've got about three or more days in the UK! Did we look into a ferry from Ireland to France?

I seem to remember that we did but it took way to long and cost way, way too much. Plus, we were broke from the theater...

Tony's Journal

June 26, 1982

We got up at four in the morning to catch the 0510 train to Dublin. We got there and missed the 1030 train to Belfast because Butch had to go to the American Express.

You know Tony, every time something happens and we miss something, it's someone else's fault. Has anyone else noticed this?

Yes, but I'm reminded of that immortal country western singer (whose name escapes me right now) who sang "Oh Lord, it's hard to be humble, when you're perfect in every way..." Since these are my views of the "facts" I'm just drawing logical conclusions to the events that made the biggest impressions on me (thank God you all had me there to keep us alive and on schedule!).

So we sat around at the station until the 1430 train. I read the book Animal Farm

Literature? You should have just asked, you could have read some of my comics.

on the way to Belfast and from there we had only about twenty minutes to get across town and catch a train to Larne. We had about two minutes to spare!

This event made a pretty big impression on us both.

Then off to Larne to catch a boat to Stranrear. From there we are taking a train to London and expect to get there tomorrow morning. Alexander Haig resigned last night and came as a shock.

Because we were all such close friends and he hadn't mentioned this to any of us.

The end of the Falkland War, Prince William's birth…and now Al? It was too much to take.

Didn't really do anything today but catch trains and that is probably what we'll be doing all day tomorrow.

Which, when you think about it, is infinitely better that MISSING trains all day.

All of us are pretty tired. My cold isn't quite as bad.

I know Dawn, ever the sympathetic one judging by her recent comments, was glad to hear it.

Actions speak louder than words. Here's a hint…still no action!

All is well in the long run and no big problems.

Who are you trying to convince here?

Oh well, here's to another night on the train.

Remember....it saves on accommodations.

Butch's Journal

Day 26 - June 26, 1982 - Cork to Dublin to Belfast to Larne, Ireland to Stranrear, Scotland

(PLEASE NOTE: There is no mention of California Bonnie ANYWHERE in this journal entry. Apparently I was over her by this point, although I'm sure the reverse was not true.)

We left at 05:10 this morning.

Do they still have a 5:10 in the morning now?

Crossed the street to the station and caught our train without a hitch.

Comforting to know we still knew how to cross the street.

Our car had a busted steam pipe in it. I couldn't get any sleep.

Does anyone else remember the busted steam pipe? It's quite vivid in my memory for some reason.

We got to Dublin about 09:00 and Susi and I made our way to the American Express office where I got my $100.

Thanks Mom!

Got it in travelers cheques and went around the corner to their competition, Thomas Cook,

See, AMEX was out of cash so they were sending everyone down to Thos. Cook to cash everything, which I thought was interesting since they were direct competitors. See? It was interesting because of that. OK, well, I thought it was interesting.

and cashed $60 worth - $20 for Susi,

Thanks Susi.

$20 for Dawn

Thanks Dawn.

and $20 for me.

Well, thank god THAT'S over....now....what can I foolishly spend this money on?

We went back to the station, on the way buying Tony's cake, Susi's Irish book, and some sardines.

There we go, that's a nice start.

Nobody offered me a sardine...and I'm pretty sure Dawn wasn't going to have any.

At the station Susi and I had some egg and chips and a half pint of Guinness.

Very good, well on the way to blowing the whole wad. (Egg and chips, sardines, Guinness......makes your mouth water just thinking about it).

Then I bought some old comic reprints

Alright, that should about do it for today.

I still have these comics by the way, just looked through them the other day. They were filled with great stuff and they were thick and they were cheap. I would love to get some more. They had classic reprints from the fifties and early 60s, mostly pre-superhero marvel and Charlton stuff, lots of Steve Ditko, Jack Kirby, Wally Wood and Joe Simon...The Giants.

and just messed around until our train came. We got on and got to Belfast with no bomb threats or nothing.

First use of a double negative in the journal entries. Do I win a prize?

When we got to Belfast we had a half-hour to get to the right station to our train to London. We made it there at 17:22, the train was supposed to leave at 17:25 (whew!).

I remember this vividly too. We were literally running, top speed, from train to bus to train. I'm sure it was a sight: Four cranky people who had got up at 4am and traveled all day, probably snapping at each other, running around with our packs, our various bags of sweaters-books-sardines, and, apparently, a cake somewhere. I would love to have a video of that scene.

We got to Larne just in time, got our tickets and got on board. I found a beer mug and took it.

That's what I needed, ANOTHER hard, bulky, breakable thing to carry around. Don't forget, I'm carrying that Guinness tankard I bought in Dublin.

Your backpack started out looking like a little knapsack thing, by then end of the trip, it looked like you were carrying another person on your back for cryin' out loud!!

We had some hot dogs and chips.

Christ on a cracker! No wonder we were tired....there's no way our blood could still have been flowing unobstructed through our veins by that point after eating so much CRAP! Didn't we ever go into a place that had maybe a salad? A turkey sandwich? Something!

Disembarked at Stranrear and got seats on a fairly crowded train.

I remember this not at all. Did we sleep upright in chairs on the train or did we get to stretch out? Perhaps I was already asleep when we boarded the train. Anyone record this?

We should get to London tomorrow morn.

I hope we can get some deep-fried food there.

A KFC on every corner!

Tony's Journal

June 27, 1982

Well, I turned 18 years old today.

How depressing is that?

More so every day.

Spent the day traveling. We got to London a little late and finally caught a train to Dover. We slept most of the way. From Dover, we caught a Sealink ship to Oostende, Belgium. On the train to Dover we celebrated my birthday with a cake. It was good.

Just shows how deadened our taste buds were from all the shit we'd been eating. Maybe not deadened, just covered with a layer of deep-fryer grease.

The ship ride took about four hours. We were gonna stay in Oostende, but decided not to.

You mention that and so do I, I wonder why we had this thing against Oostende?

It looked a lot like Spain to me.

Instead we took the next train 15 minutes to Brugge where we *are staying for BF 185 ($4.00) in the Europa Jugendhedre which includes showers and a breakfast. Not bad and it is a nice looking place, very clean. Probably as good, if not better, than the one we stayed in at Zurich.*

That one in Zurich was nice but I think the setting made this one even better.

Like I say, we didn't really do anything but travel. We were hoping to get to Amsterdam, but we'll have to wait till tomorrow.

At least you recorded it.

Everybody is happy, I think, that we'll be home soon.

Everyone except Dawn I think. I seem to remember her wanting to go on well into July she was having such a good time.

True. She had enough money to buy us all a month's rail pass extension.

So long.

Butch's Journal

Day 27 - June 27, 1982 - London-Dover, England to Oostende-Brugge, Belgium [Tony's B-day]

Happy Birthday buddy. (It is still on this date isn't it? It hasn't changed in 15 years has it?)

Thank you. Yep, it's still today. Except now I'm 33 years old. Oh boy...

Got to London a little late. We found out we had to take a different ferry than expected to Amsterdam, another 6.00 pounds so I had to cash another $20.00.

Interrail trip tip #987: Ferries = hemorrhaging money

Those babies were one of those hidden costs we sure didn't count on. Now do you realize that London was our most frequently visited destination on the whole trip? This is the third time we've gone through London central to get somewhere else.

Got a Casy Jones hamburger and some more comics.

Ever the thrifty (and healthy!) one.

Forsaking Burger King...tsk, tsk. And what? No KFC?

The train we tried to catch first wasn't the one we could take, it was a hydro-foil, ours left 2 hours later. So we messed around until then. Then we couldn't find a place to sit but finally got a compartment, in 1st class, by ourselves.

A strike starting in less than 24 hours, people leaving the UK in droves, scrambling to leave, hanging on the outside of the trains....and we get a 1st class compartment to ourselves. Had I been conscious I probably would have been insulted.

I wonder why we didn't have to pay a surcharge or something.

We gave Tony his cake and slept.

Lord knows where this cake has been. I really have no memory of where we could have possibly kept it. We've had it now for over 24 hours, we've been crammed into various trains and running to catch trains and busses. I really don't know how this could have been any good...but I do remember us eating it...just before passing out. "Countryside? Screw the countryside, I need some sleep."

It must have been made of weapons grade wheat or something. I just hope it wasn't close to the nappy underwear.

We got to Dover, got on the ship, I got another mug.

See, they WANT you to take them...it's like the towels in hotels...they WANT you to take them because they're free advertising...see?

You must be up to about 35 pounds worth of beer mugs by now. No wonder we're starting to think about heading home.

Ate a little, I got 3 bottles of Becks, Tony got a Stella Artois.

Good lord! No wonder this entry is a little choppy. I was obviously writing it once we got to Brugge and, apparently, by that time I would

have been hung over. 3 Becks! What the hell was I thinking? I can barely do that now!

It seems like we were always pretty eager to try the local brews, although Becks isn't exactly local to London or Belgium, but who cares when you're 18 and have money to burn. Plus, it probably took away the hunger pangs.

> We got to Oostende, couldn't find a place to stay so we took the 15 minute ride to Brugge, gave a call to the IYHF, caught the bus, got to the hostel, had something hot to drink then went right to bed.

I remember this IYHF being really nice, quiet, cozy, and clean. It didn't have that dorm atmosphere. In fact, if I recall correctly, Tony and I were in a double room...isn't that right? I hope your entries are a little more in depth than mine. I think I was a little brain dead from the last 40 hours of train/boat travel.

I recollect that the place was nice, but I don't recall the double room set up all that much. This 40 hour trek really did us in. We had about three days left on our pass, but I know we're starting to think about packing it in, no pun intended.

For the most part my journal ends here....but I do have something for tomorrow so I won't say anymore until then.

No way, well, I go to the bitter end, plus I have a post script later in the year kind of summing things up. More on that when we get there. However, my last official entry of the trip will be Sunday...stay tuned.

HAPPY BIRTHDAY TONY!

Thanks again. I still have my old passport from the trip and I'm fond of it because of this day in particular. I got an exit stamp in

England and an entry stamp for Belgium, on my birthday. I thought that was cool. I've also got receipts for the Pound 6.00 ferry ride on Sealink and for the youth hostel.

Tony's Journal

June 28, 1982

> *We left Brugge in the morning for Amsterdam. We had to change trains in Antwerpen.*

I don't remember that.

Our breakfast consisted of three slices of bread, butter, jam, cheese, ginger snaps, and some milk. It was good.

Pretty good description there Tone, I do which you hadn't been quite so vague as to what TYPES of bread, jam, and cheese we ate. I don't remember this either, where did we get this bounteous repast? Was it supplied by the IYHF or did someone think we were beggars and give us some food?

> *We got the train and changed in Antwerp. But not before having a quick Hot Dog.*

Because Breakfast was far, far too healthy.

> *We decided on the train that everyone wanted to go home tonight, pretty much, from Amsterdam.*

OK, fess up, what does the "pretty much" mean? You didn't want to go home? I seem to recall wanting to hit one more country, as my mother pointed out when I forwarded her my entry, I still had about

$30 left....shoot, I could go another two weeks on that.

I think we were weighing the option of scratching out a few more days of our trip, we had paid for the month you know, and getting the hell home! The bodies were willing, but our minds said, "No Way."

So, we got to Amsterdam and checked our luggage. From there we walked to the Anne Frank Huis. It was very interesting although it was my second visit. I got to lead us there since I sort of knew where it was.

Wasn't that nice of me to let you lead? Thought I'd throw you a bone since it was our last day and all.

After we saw that, we walked to a McDonald's where we pigged out.

Certainly unlike what we did at every other fast food place we went.

Dawn wasn't feeling too well though.

I can't imagine. Look at the shit we've had to eat just TODAY!

From there, the girls walked back to the station & Butch and I went to buy some beer for the long trip back to Munich.

I don't remember if we found any or not...did we?

Of course we did. I think we scored about a twelve pack worth of St. Pauli girl (isn't that the biggie Dutch beer?) It was in green bottles.

Now we have a compartment to ourselves which is good.

That happens a lot. We must smell so fine.

Susi for sure is going to Augsburg to visit her OMA, Butch probably is tagging along, Dawn's thinking about it, I don't really want to, but will if Dawn does I guess.

You should have gone. We didn't go to a McDonalds or Burger King or Dunkin' Donuts or anything but it was still a pretty good time.

This will be about a twelve hour ride, but not our longest trip.

Twelve hours? Hell, we could do twelve hours standing on our heads by this time (which I think we did at one point).

Now I can think back on the trip and overall I had a lot of fun. I feel it was well worth the experience and wish I could do it every year.

Amen.

We had a lot of good times and only a few bad.

Other than a few inconveniences I don't recall any real "bad times" at all. Of course, that be the rosy shades that 15 years will strap on your hindsight.

Even those weren't all that bad. I think the four of us did good considering we were in such close quarters for about a month.

Really....however, notice that it was the last time you and I have spent any real time together for 15 years so maybe it had more effect than we thought.

The cities were all interesting and I don't think I would want to change any of the trip.

The 28th day of the trip would be an unfortunate time to be bringing it up anyway bucko.

I'll sum up later after I've had time to think.

Why didn't you tell me you were doing that? I wish I would have thought to do that! I gave you that great postcard idea and you didn't share the "summing up" idea!

So long.

And so, this marks the end of my trip journal. I do have a post script I'll send on tomorrow.

U.S.A

7. № 94878

Data	27/6/82	Totalen
NO	185	185 –
N		
W		
O		
LP		
LA		
K		
S		
Tot.		185

JEUGDHERBERG
BRUGGE
Baron Ruzettelaan 143
8320 - Tel. 050 - 35.26.79
28 JUNI 1982

Butch's Journal

Day 28 - June 28.1982 - Brugge, Belgium to ...

...

And that's it, that's all I wrote for that day, I think it was the stop off at Susi's Oma's house that sort of knocked me out of synch there. Which is a shame because I remember some of the things about Amsterdam, but I don't remember them all. I remember walking through the red light district and seeing the hookers in the little "self-serve" booths (actually, when Melanie and I went back a few years ago we stayed right around the corner from those exact same brothels), I remember the Anne Frank House, the train station, some Heineken

Heineken! That was it, not St. Pauli Girl...very important to distinguish.

and that's about it. There is a postcard however:

POSTCARD: "A nice montage" of Brugge on the front, none of the stuff I remember seeing on that trip. Really cool stamp with a star and a rainbow and a city on a hill....really cool. I wrote:

> #17 June 28, 1982
> Traveled for last 39 hours - 2 ferry rides - got to Oostend - Didn't want tostay there - came to Brugge - Nice place - I've been here before - Leave for Amsterdam today - then home

Not much there I know but it's something. Susi and I did go to her Oma's house in Augsburg, you guys didn't. We spent the night there and came back to Munich the next day. HOWEVER, I have no memory of where I stayed after that. Was I still living with you Tony? (Editor's Note: Butch lived with Tony's family for the senior year of high school so as to remain in Germany to finish school. Something for which he has always been, and still is, eternally grateful.) **I mean, I doubt I would have had the time to pack everything up before we left, but, I don't recall ever packing anything up EVER. Where was I? I remember going to the 4th of July gathering in Perlacher, but that's really my only post trip, pre-airport memory. Can anyone help me out here?**

You know, it was a blur for me too. I don't think you came back to the house Butch. I had to go to my daily journal to see what happened. You guys got back from Augsburg and we went to the Little O'Fest a couple of times. Beer and chicken (not KFC) ruled the day. You spent one more night at my house and eventually flew back to the States around the 5th of July. Dawn blew her remaining travel bucks on an Atari game system (she's always been an early adopter). Me, Dawn and Susi went to one last going away party, got toasted, toasted you and within a few days, I was following you to the States.

I feel like I should sum up here: I would say that the trip was one of the pivotal events in my life, and it came at just the right time. The dry run Tony and I took to Italy (actually, there was nothing dry about that run as I recall) was NOTHING compared to this trip. I too, would repeat it every year if I could.

Blatt 5

Kontrolle	Datum	Von	nach
LINK TRAVEL LTD. HUDSONS PLACE VICTORIA STATION 3 LONDON	27 JUL 1982	LONDON	BRUGGE
		über DOVER OOSTENDE	
	28.06.82	BRUGGE	AMSTERDAM
		über Antwerpen	Rotterdam
	29.06.82	AMSTERDAM	MÜNCHEN
		über	
	29.06.82	München Hbf	FASANGARTEN
		über	
		über	

Headed home.

Tony's Journal

November 24, 1982

Well, it has been four months since Inter Rail '82

Actually, hasn't it been 5 months? (or 15 years?)

Well, I was only a freshman in college. I guess they better check my math test scores. I was able to waive all math requirements because of the excellent education I got at MAHS, but I couldn't count past five or so.

You know, they must have had good math (if there is such a thing) at MAHS because not only did I place out of my math requirement freshman year, the math prof said it was the best placement test score he'd ever seen....so, with that obvious push into math and science I became a liberal arts god!!!! Morde sortum.

DAWN: Alright, alright — enough about the math waivers you braggarts. You had to be a monkey not to place out of it in college, O.K?

Is Cheeta trying to tell us she didn't waive out of her math classes?

and I have had a lot of time to think about it. Looking back, it has to be one of the defining, fun filled, experiences of my life.

It sure was, and, looking back has been a fun experience as well.

I agree, once again, with the gentleman from Virginia.

DAWN: Yes, I've come around fellas! I have to say that our trip was by far my most wonderful life experience (except for child birth, of course, which ranks right up there with folding socks.) Thank you both so much for sharing your journals. I thought perhaps if you were interested, I could start mine from the beginning now.

> *It was well worth it and I definitely want to do it again in a year or so.*

Did you ever? The closest I came was in 91 when Melanie and I went from Nuremburg to Amsterdam by train. I pretty much realized at that point that I wasn't 17 anymore (not that I hadn't had a few clues before that time). We were crammed into the hallway going because the train was packed, and into a compartment with some Eurailers coming back and I got to thinking how much time we had spent on the train on the first trip. We practically lived on it. Amazing.

Let's see, I've only been back to Germany once, and that was the summer after my freshman year at Pierce. My dad had my old job at the gas station lined up for me (and I was looking forward to some good old idle time) and the closest I got to travel was a drive down to B.A. to visit JoAnn for an afternoon. My dad, however, took off for Yugoslavia for a week while I was slaving at the gas station! What's up with that??

What's up with that? That's your-dad-getting-away-from-the-kid-whose-sucking-up-all-his-money-going-to-that-hoity-toity-New-England-school-who-needs-a-lesson-in-where-that-dough-is-coming-from is what that is.

DAWN: I took an "International Business" class in college

with Professor ? (Tony, what was that marketing guy's name?) and we traveled to many countries. Mainly, I went to relive our trip and to show everyone where we had been and what we had done. I even took my journal! I thought it would be just as much fun. Let me tell you....it was not! I think it was the crowd I was with....more interested in partying than furthering their cultural experience (well, maybe that's ok sometimes). Tony, how could you have let me hang out with those people? Plus we spent umpteen days in Frankfurt, of all places. This professor would not let me go to Munich by myself....even for a day! I was quite miffed!

> *It was super. I don't have any regrets at all. It was a tremendous learning experience also. All the places, people, and things I got to see was incredible.*

I don't know about you but I bragged about it in college for years and years and years (of course, I was in college for years and years and years).

I always find a way to work it into a conversation. You're at a party, talking about the Irish 'trouble' (this is Boston you know), I pop in and tell them how we almost got blown up by a mad IRA bomber on our desperate escape from the oppression that is Ulster, when I was only 17. Then, I make my way to the Cheese Nips while everyone comments about how worldly I am. I'll throw a reference in about our Italian trip, or London, then off to the Buffalo wings…everyone hates me by the end of these get togethers.

I'm surprised it takes them until the end.

DAWN: Yeah, I've come across a few people who did a trip similar to ours, only different countries. Well...then...I guess it wouldn't be a trip similar to ours then, would it?

Well, cheese nips and buffalo wings, I see that the inter rail diet is something you've managed to maintain over the years.

It's only because there are just not enough KFC's around here, I'm telling you! But, Dunkin Donuts? You can't throw a rock without hitting one.

> *I know as time goes on it will be harder to find the time to do this again,*

Pretty insightful for a college freshman. I pretty much thought at the time I would be able to do it every summer.

Yeah, I was torn between a philosophy major or some business major. Then I remembered how hungry I was on that trip and decided I didn't want to spend my life in train stations begging for food so I majored in some hokey Comp Sci thing they had going.

Well, let me say *this* about *that*: Well, there's really nothing I can say. But, if nothing else, my philosophy degree has allowed me to find the wisdom in begging for food. (and my field isn't scrambling to figure out what's going to happen in 2 and a half years when the clocks read "00"...have fun)

DAWN: And I am able to see how the benefit received from begging for food far outweighs the cost of buying it (or something like that - I still don't have that principles of accounting stuff down yet).

> *but it must be done. It's hard to explain, it was great.*
> *TS*

I'm very struck by how upbeat you were here. Early in your freshman year, I had screwed you over by not coming to FPC and being too

embarrassed to tell you AND you and Dawn were breaking up at some point here weren't you? I remember some letters and phone calls from about this time but I don't think you ever sounded THIS upbeat. That's great, I'm glad it was as great a memory for you as it was for me..now if we could work on Dawn...

Yep, that's me, singing and dancing while my world is crashing down all around me. It's why today I own stock in Tums.

And what about those kidney stones, I seem to remember kidney stones (by the way, I don't know any philosophy majors with a Tums addiction...draw your own conclusions).

I was home for the first major break at school, Thanksgiving break. I didn't have to work at the gas station and my mom wasn't charging me rent for my room at home yet, so I was livin' large. It was a good time, and since time blunts all the bad times, it's only going to get better and better.

Yeah, let's see how great it is in another 15 years when we do it again.

Dawn will come around too, if she hasn't already. I don't think she had that bad a time on the trip, did you Dawn?

DAWN: As I said before....most wonderful experience. Thanks guys!

Appendix

The Ezbit

There are a number of mentions of "the Ezbit" within the journal commentary, though seldom in the journal entries themselves, which is remarkable due only to how useful it turned out to be. This section is designed to give you a better idea of the Ezbit.

The Ezbit was a camp stove that Tony bought in Munich to take on the trip and he remembers little about why he chose that one. Stories we have heard since say that it is German military issue with a consumer version sold in camp stores. We are unsure if it is even manufactured anymore.

In the following pictures you will see the Ezbit go from its compact state to its ready-to-use state. The playing card is for size comparison.

Compact...about the size of a deck of cards.

The grill snaps off...

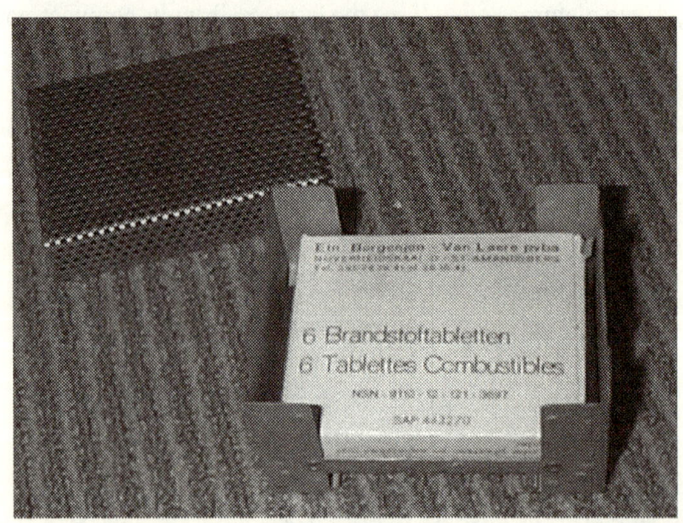

...and the stove folds open to reveal the box of fuel tablets..

...one fuel tablet is placed in the center of the storage area.

The grill is replaced over the fuel tablet.

*The fuel is lit, and the stove is ready to cook a hot (well...*warm *anyway) camp meal.*

4

www.ingramcontent.com/pod-product-compliance
Lightning Source LLC
Chambersburg PA
CBHW051754040426
42446CB00007B/356

* 9 7 8 0 9 7 5 9 7 3 7 2 1 *